# Don't Look Back

## Vol. 1

### 40 Selected Articles, Essays and Q&As

# Don't Lose Track
## Vol. 1

40 Selected Articles, Essays and Q&As

Jordannah Elizabeth

Winchester, UK
Washington, USA

First published by Zero Books, 2016
Zero Books is an imprint of John Hunt Publishing Ltd., Laurel House, Station Approach,
Alresford, Hants, SO24 9JH, UK
office1@jhpbooks.net
www.johnhuntpublishing.com
www.zero-books.net

For distributor details and how to order please visit the 'Ordering' section on our website.

Text copyright: Jordannah Elizabeth 2015

ISBN: 978 1 78535 193 8
Library of Congress Control Number: 2015946054

A CIP catalogue record for this book is available from the British Library.

Design: Lee Nash

Printed and bound by CPI Group (UK) Ltd, Croydon, CR0 4YY, UK

We operate a distinctive and ethical publishing philosophy in all
areas of our business, from our global network of authors to
production and worldwide distribution.

# CONTENTS

Foreword by Mark Fritz                                          viii

Preface                                                          1

An Exclusive: Five POVs on Gentrification in America             5

Section One: Music Reviews                                       15

Section Two: Columns                                             35

Section Three: Essays, Series and Profiles                       59

Section Four: Best-Of Lists and Favorite Picks                   77

Section Five: Interviews                                         93

Thank Yous and Acknowledgements                                  132

*This book is dedicated to:*

*My Grandmother*
*Annie McFadden*

*My Grandmother*
*Veryl L. Harvey*

*My Great Aunt*
*Daisy Granger*

*My Mother*
*Susan L. Phillips*

*Harriet Tubman*

*and to all the women and little girls*
*who the world has seemingly rejected and overlooked.*
*I do it all for you.*

# Foreword by Mark Fritz

How can you not love somebody who writes a column, and lists the pertinent songs, for a mixtape to accompany a first-time sexual encounter? Someone who extols the economic virtues of pet-sitting, or explains the practical advantages of living in a so-called "AirB&B?" Jordannah Elizabeth writes about these things and so much more, wittily deconstructing all aspects of life and love and, most of all, art.

I wrote a couple of pieces for Publik/Private, a website that Jordannah runs. It is offbeat, original and quite beautiful, very much like Jordannah herself. Her love of the written word delivered in a visceral way is infectious and inspiring. Her commitment to raw passion and the uninhibited expression of human emotion has made me fiercely loyal to this wonderfully complex artist. I take great pride in the fact that she is my editor.

The things that I, as well as my writing partner, Joyce Riha Linik, wrote for Jordannah perhaps would not be published elsewhere. One piece I wrote was a meditation on Monica Lewinsky (I had a double date involving this sadly ridiculed human being). It examined a life that continued after the circus of media attention had moved on. Joyce and I collaborated on another piece that was essentially a vivid and explicit depiction of a sexual encounter. Joyce also wrote a short story about a boyfriend so obsessed with finding a Yeti—the Abominable Snowman, the so-called Bigfoot—that he actually began morphing into such a creature. Not only did Jordannah embrace these pieces with enthusiasm, her layouts and her choice of art to accompany each were both brilliant and elegant yet somehow earthy, which, again, is probably a good way to describe Ms. Elizabeth herself. (The sex story that Joyce and I wrote was accompanied by two people with hand grenades for heads, a perfect image for a piece about the primal power of unbridled lust.)

I've never met Jordannah in the physical sense. But, and I guess it's a testament to the power of communications technology, our message exchanges and telephone conversations revealed somebody who was bracingly frank, freakishly smart, beguilingly charming and pretty damn hilarious. I tested her with a few outrageous comments, which she fielded with aplomb and then fired whistling rejoinders right back at me. As I mentioned earlier, this charismatic woman engenders a fierce allegiance.

As for this book: Reading the selections in this volume supports my own gut instincts about this unique woman. Though our relationship is based purely on her role as purveyor of original writing, I was only superficially aware of her involvement in the other arts. Now I understand the diversity of her creative genius. And I can only marvel at her evocative writing. Like all great writers, it has a singularly distinctive voice that seems almost effortless. It is by turns muscular and powerful, droll and beautiful. It is mesmerizing and addictive. It is funny and just sexy as hell.

Jordannah, herself an accomplished composer and singer of haunting songs, writes primarily about culture in general and music in particular. This is fitting, because she writes with beats and rhythms and a cadence that sweep the reader along like a really good song. Her music reviews, interviews and essays about life as we know it are as eclectic as her own artistic tastes, the result of a questing mind unencumbered by boundaries. It's impossible not to both admire her work, and also genuinely *like* the person who wrote this stuff. The sheer breadth of her music reviews is dazzling; country, punk, hip-hop, psychedelic and pure pop are dealt with deftly, and Jordannah has an uncanny knack for drilling down into what seems like a perfectly logical analysis of the psyche of a particular artist. Her broad range of knowledge allows her to find something that eludes lesser writers: the intersection where not just genres, but ideas, somehow meet to form something original. And that, I guess, is who Jordannah Elizabeth is: somebody who lives at the crossroads of virtually every component of contemporary culture.

Check out this compact excerpt of a concert review for the *San Francisco Bay Guardian*. The nuance, the sense of place, is so evocative that you can almost smell this particular moment in time:

> *While the hazy, eerie atmosphere coated the venue, LA's Giant Drag was able to play a sensually dark set of songs, completely appropriate for the early evening. The crowd slowly trickled in throughout the night, not quite filling the room, and people seemed to shift and cycle through the venue, never standing in one place for too long. There was never a moment where there was a complete loss of the crowd's attention, but there was a quiet level of distraction going on.*

She closes with this:

> *Everything seemed to flow peacefully as the show ended with the songs "New Teenage Mutilation," "Sweet 69" and "The Last Dance." McBean played solo for the last song, and it was endearing and really lovely to watch—until McBean suddenly smashed his guitar over his amp, hurling it over his head several times until it cracked, ending the show on a strangely violent note.*
> 
> *The band had joined him on stage seconds before McBean attacked his guitar, and they put their instruments down just as quickly as they had picked them up after McBean walked past them leaving the stage. The rest of Pink Mountaintops mingled with the crowd, seeming unaffected by McBean's behavior, allowing their non-inner circle to slowly disperse from the evening's odd occurrence. The show was weird, but the band is great.*

I guess the things I find most endearing are the personal essays, the meditations on love and life. Her lyrically instructional series of essays on "How to Survive as a Broke-Ass Writer" in particular resonated deeply with me because that's exactly what I am. I've spent the past year crashing on couches and in my car during a road trip from Key West to LA to Detroit, where I'm homesteading a derelict house because it's the cheapest way to live and write.

*So, I've been on the road as a writer and musician for a little over a decade. The first time I officially became homeless I was 19 years old, and the first time I ran away from home was at age 15. I have always been a transient person. Working and moving has been my life, and I chose a career that allows me to travel often. As a journalist, I've flown from coast to coast to get interviews and exclusive tours of studios by my favorite artists.*

*Nonetheless, traveling, subletting, and couch and hostel surfing is not easy. Finding a place to rest your head every night can be a challenge when you're living from freelance check to freelance check. Now that I am almost 30, I have the financial means to negotiate costs for room and board and sublets.*

*Don't get me wrong, if you're making less than $1,000 a month, this article is not for you. This article is for broke-ass writers who work, receive wages for what they do and have wiggle room to get around and find temporary living situations that enable them to do their jobs well.*

This beautiful book is so many things that I guess I'll close with the least romantic aspect about it: It is laced with so much practical, common-sense insight about the artistic life that I really wish it had been written years ago so I could have learned her lessons. But, hell, I doubt if I would have loved it any more than I do right now.

How can anybody who writes for a living not utterly adore somebody who opens a column with this?

*If you're a writer, it probably means you're a moody introspective introverted dork. I mean that in the kindest and most affectionate of ways, because I am one of you.*

—*Pulitzer Prize winner Mark Fritz, author of* Permanent Deadline *and* Lost on Earth.

# Preface

This is the third time I've written this dern preface. "Dern" is a backwoods version of the word "damn" that my mother used often when I was a little girl. The purified version of this word did not stop my grandmother from cracking up with laughter every time my mother exclaimed "DERN!" whenever she'd do something like bang her shin or become frustrated with some random quagmire. My grandmother, laughing with tears in her eyes, would still accuse her of cursing even though she clearly did not.

I guess if I'm going to mention the word "dern," I should also bring up my mother's go-to road-rage insult, "idjit!" Most would think "idjit" is not a real word, but if you look it up in the urban dictionary, it will read clear as day: "One of Yosemite Sam's catchphrases used to describe a Stupid Idiot Dragon, or used to describe Bugs Bunny." For as long as I can remember, whenever someone cut my mother off in traffic, should coin the driver at fault "IDJIT!" That's the lady who gave birth to me.

I remember a few years ago when I was hanging out with my father, he'd taken me to lunch and I was gossiping about myself to him. I was describing a young man my friend was trying to hook me up with in Brooklyn, NY and I began to ramble, "He keeps talking about this person named Taylor..." My dad wisely replied, "Do you think he had a thing with her?" Completely taken off-guard I asked, "How did you know Taylor was a girl?"

He replied, "Taylor Swift. DUH!"

These are my parents... so if you think me being a cheeky pop-culture writer was all my idea, I have to tell you, I can't take much credit for the weirdo I was born to be. The combination of my father's fascination with current affairs, sports, box office movies and music, and my mom's highly fierce intelligence, combined with constant "Lucille Ball-like" reactions to things

1

just kind of pushed me forward in life to have the charmed gift of making people think, laugh and react in ways they did not expect to react.

I don't have a formal educational degree, but I have a PhD in individualism and irony.

I didn't speak much until I was about 17 years old. I was deathly shy and daydreamed so much that reality scared the hell out of me. I would get so overwhelmed by my large extended-family gatherings, I would sit in closets just to get a rest from the activity. I was not very beautiful when I was young so I read a lot. Mark Fritz describes me as "beautiful," but my looks just kind of happened. I do very little to maintain them. I use a facial moisturizer and a mud mask once a week and I eat ok. I walk instead of ride in cars to maintain a healthy figure. I have to do those things now that I am close to 30 years old but before that I did nothing. I've always done what I've wanted to do. I don't try to push people to help me, I don't really rely on anything but my imagination and it's always been that way. People let me alone well enough, and because of that I have a freedom that allows me to acutely concentrate on my dreams and my writing. Because people give me space to create, the manifestations of my dreams are things I am happy to openly share with the world.

This book is a manifestation of a dream. I've worked 14-hour days since I was 17 to prepare for this book. I never finished a degree because every time I got enough education and equilibrium to complete a project I had been working on in my mind, I'd drop out and go live life and use the practical knowledge I learned from school to build a project, concept or service I could be paid to enact. Does this life pattern make me a flake? I'm not sure. I think I'm a bit more like a freak. You see, I don't know how to conform. I don't know what it feels like to want to work 9 to 5 job or maintain a romantic relationship where my lover is available more than 3 to 6 months out of the year. I don't know what it's like to want to have a child without having financially security... or at the very least emotional security. The "American Dream" (or the "Western World Dream"): I've never once in my life gave a shit about it... Therefore, I am a freak... Because I am an American, and I'm supposed to act like one. I just want to write. The right lover, the children that are meant to be born of my loins and a beautiful home will all meet up with me in this life when the moment is right. I don't concern myself with fateful issues. I believe if you love something, let it go. If it returns it was always yours. I believe that you can be physically separated from someone, but become closer than ever with them in your mind and heart while they are away. Fuck telephones and technology. I use my heart, and I send messages through my art and writing.

Anyway, in the next few pages, you will read a bit of what I've written over the past few years or so. I believe the earliest work dates back to 2011 when I wrote a couple of pieces for the *Colorado Springs Independent*. I was fired from that paper. I was fired from a couple of publications that are included in this book, but this fact is of course no hindrance to the relevance of the articles, which I humbly hope stand the test of time.

\* \* \*

Not that I am particularly concerned, but I know what critics are going to say. They're going to say that this book doesn't have a "thesis" and the content is too "diverse." But I don't see it that way.

In this book you'll find a short quip about Blaze Foley's noble and tragic death, a piece on how Ishmael Butler has a nonchalant awareness of the existence of *Lese Majeste*, and an article about women fighting for the right to go topless in public in New York City.

My advice when reading this book: don't think so much. Let these reviews, essays, columns and interviews peak your sense of adventure and imagination. Have a bit of fun. Let your sense of curiosity guide you and read this book with wonderment at what's going to be on the next page. Ok?

Every human being I have covered is a human being who reflects the truest essence of integrity, brilliance and humility. Every human being I have written about has inspired me in some way to be greater and to live larger. I hope you will discover new music from this book, and I hope you will embark on a long-term relationship with the art of the artists featured in this collection.

You and me? We're going to do this again really soon. Whether I'm writing a novel, another anthology, a how-to book or a comic, I hope we will experience life together through the printed word for many years down the line. Just understand that I make mistakes and if you and I meet, I may disappoint you, but through these pages, let's connect and accept one another, fully and unconditionally as you, the reader, and me, the writer.

We'll go on a journey of exploration of sound and the uncovering of truth.

One last thing:

Love one another. Please be kind to the less fortunate. Please love your parents and kids and shower them with jokes and embraces. Cross bridges for your friends… because you get what you give. We all need love.

.je

# An Exclusive:
# Five POVs on Gentrification in America

*(An unpublished article on Gentrification and Race in America.)*
*I worked on this piece in the aftermath of the Baltimore riots. I felt*
*helpless because I was in San Francisco and my hometown was*
*burning to the ground. I had a lot of questions about the changes*
*America was going through and why Black men (and women) were*
*being targeted and mistreated by American police forces. This is a*
*raw look at the answers I received. The intro is raw as well.*
*Sometimes, as a journalist, you have to do what you have to do and*
*say what you have to say in a world that tries to force writers to*
*push everything through a constructed voice and filter that is not*
*truly our own. There's nothing wrong with rules, but I don't*
*always have to do things the way people tell me. Money is not my*
*goal. Giving people a realistic and authentic perspective is*
*something I'm very interested in doing for the rest of my life.*

\* \* \*

The Merriam-Webster dictionary defines gentrification as "the
process of renewal and rebuilding accompanying the influx of
middle-class or affluent people into deteriorating areas that
often displaces poorer residents." This definition doesn't explain
where gentrification takes place, but the word is mainly tied to
the American cultural and political infrastructure. The issue may
only truly be appealing to liberals and social activists who incor-
porate the poor and working class into their professional and
social causes, but I would like to highlight the subtler cultural
manifestations that are growing from this, as Saul Williams and
Porter Ray explain it, "cyclical migration algorithm."

The one thing that truly connects the men who spoke with me
for this article is that gentrification has affected their lives in

direct manners. Whether this means being denied housing by landlords, or journalistically covering an inner-city uprising, or just watching their best friend survive systemic social exclusion because of their financial bracket and skin color, they all have a story to tell about gentrification and what it has done to them and their cities.

Something to think about:

*New York Times* broke the news that for the first time in recorded history, the suicide of Black children between 5 and 11 years old has not only risen, but has doubled and exceeded the rate of white child suicide in America between 1993 and 2012.

The groundbreaking murder case of 17-year-old Trayvon Martin quietly brought on the emergence of the neo civil rights era, in which Ferguson became the manifestation of the growing agitation stemming from the not-guilty verdict of George Zimmerman. This led to the Baltimore uprising that seemed to be the final break in the levy of the American poor's exasperation at the imbalance of American race culture due to systemic police brutality, heartless abuse and the destruction and reconstruction of their neighborhood occurring without regard for the effect it would have on their families and lives.

This commentary is not geared to do anything but open the floor for five artists to tell their stories. Every answer is unique, every man is unique and they all range in age, race and profession. I just had a thought that maybe if we stop talking for a second and really listen, we can find pearls of reality that we can all relate to.

### Joe Talbot, Producer of *The Last Black Man in San Francisco*, on his best friend Jimmie Fails, San Francisco, CA

[Jimmie and I] met on the border of Mission and Bernal Heights. After Jimmie lost his house, he moved around a lot and ended up in a housing project that was up the street from where I grew up.

At that point in the city, there were white kids from Bernal Heights who only hung out with other white kids, but there was a significant amount of us who didn't. All of my earliest memories are of hanging out with lots of different kinds of kids from our neighborhood. All my first friends and girlfriends didn't look like me and didn't have the same background as I did. I would run around the neighborhood with a high 8 camera and make short films. I'd grab any kid I could to be in the films, and Jimmie was one of those kids.

My fear is that our friendship would not be able to exist in the future San Francisco. I think that should be horrifying to a lot of people. My parents wanted me to grow up having experiences with other people. Latino, Black and white kids would stumble from different parts of town to hang out in Precita Park and friendships were inevitably formed, but now Precita Park is very different.

I think it's really interesting to watch how the lack of a Black middle class affects both white and Black people. For white people, they only see "ghetto Black people" and they equate ghetto and Black as synonymous with one another. That's a really interesting problem here. I talk to my white friends who grew up in San Francisco who think this and I cringe when they say it because they clearly don't understand what they're talking about.

On the flip side, I have Black friends who grew up in Hunter's Point and didn't know there were white people in San Francisco until they were teenagers. Many of my friends had this debilitating fear that if they stepped outside of a specific box of what "being Black" was they would be called "white-washed" and made fun of constantly. Jimmie and I talked about this a lot. With this film, we want to show a complex person. All the things that make Jimmie wonderful to me, this archetypal San Franciscan, who's complicated—he's in the hood but he skateboards, he's an atheist but a hopeless romantic, he's obsessed with San Francisco history, etc.—he's able to operate in these different worlds and touch many different kinds of people.

In the film, Jimmie has the impossible dream of buying his old house back in San Francisco. I think there is a political statement in whether he gets the house back or not. I think if we have Jimmie get the house back we're saying: "If you work really hard you can [do anything]," and I don't think that's necessarily true right now. I think you can work your ass off and be in Jimmie's position and not get the house partially because they don't want him to get the house.

Even if he did get it back, the heartbreaking thing would be that it wouldn't be his neighborhood anymore, and everything that made the house beautiful would be gutted at this point, and remodeled, changing all the beautiful details it once had.

I think there is genuine good-hearted liberalism here and I think there are a lot of people who are just as fucked up on race as in parts of the Deep South, and they don't hide it well. I think that there are people who harbor racist sentiments and they learn through "proper education" how not to talk about these things.

I think the new racism is denying that racism exists.

**Solution:** Overnight, the tech industry could be loved in San Francisco. Invest some money in Hunter's Point and teach young people how to become young sustainable techies. Tech literacy is the new form of literacy.

## Saul Williams, Poet Actor Writer Activist, New York City, NY

I came to New York [from Paris] in July of 2013 knowing that my kids would arrive in the middle of August, so I had a month to find a place. I looked at over 30 apartments and got turned down by three apartments in Brooklyn. My realtor told me they [the landlords] were not interested in artists. They had a choice between taking three students in a three-bedroom apartment or me in family mode. They figured with three students they would have six parents, thus having six co-signers who would be responsible for the kids rather than having us [my family] who would be responsible. They chose students over families and artists.

I arrived with book deals and record deals. I had shit to show that I could afford an apartment. I wasn't welcomed in Brooklyn which was crazy. As a last resort I was looking at Harlem and was pleasantly surprised by the size of the apartments and by the response of the landlords who said, "We'll take you."

How do I feel about New York? There's an article floating around that exposed a Brooklyn landlord's practices. The piece talks about how they consciously try to not accept people of color into buildings, how they try to price them out. I'm moving in July for that same reason. My rent has gone up almost 50% in the 2 years that I've been here, so I have to leave.

I think the problem is 100% Bloomberg. Bloomberg was essentially out of touch with the people and their responses. When the richest man in New York becomes the mayor of New York, there's a problem. It's very similar to George Washington who, before he was President, was the largest land-owner and the richest man on the continent, thus becoming President. That is the story of Washington and that is the story of Bloomberg and New York.

There are different ways of looking at gentrification. You have to acknowledge that every generation sees it happen. My father grew up in Brownsville in the 1940s. He talked about how the community was very diverse and Jewish men were there raising goats and chickens in the neighborhood and Caribbeans were living there. Go to Brownsville now and it ain't mixed. Changes occur in cycles. On one hand I think we have new terms like gentrification to approach old algorithms. I think gentrification is an algorithm of migration. My great grandfather lived in Williamsburg for 50 years, up until the day he died two years ago. Williamsburg is certainly not like it was.

**Solution:** What I really think about gentrification is that the filter we put things through is Black but I really think it's about the poor. What I would like to see more of is squatters: people who take abandoned buildings and go to the state and say "Hey, we need shelter. This place is abandoned and we have every right to be here. You can't kick us out until the bank or someone purchases this building."

## Baynard Woods, Editor-at-Large of *Baltimore City Paper*, Baltimore, MD

It's interesting because people say that there isn't gentrification in Baltimore, but that's not true. There are certain areas [in Baltimore] that have changed tremendously as money pours in. Money will follow money. Station North [arts district] over the last couple of years has changed on the North Ave. side. Poorer artists are getting forced out towards the west side of town. So, small galleries are now opening over there.

That's a precursor to the city investing money into North Station and trying to attract families, but the artists who actually start the gentrification [by starting small businesses] eventually get pushed out themselves. Families are mainly getting pushed out from Greenmount West and, of course, the east side where John Hopkins University is completely taking over entire areas as they've been doing for the last several decades.

What's interesting is that in Greenmount West people actually want people to move into the houses around them because if you have a vacant house on either side of you, you can't get homeowner's insurance. More than the gentrification, the problem in Baltimore is the massive disinvestment in certain areas. It's not that rents are going up, it's that services are going down. Water is being cut off right now all throughout the city because of the way city and corporate money is flowing. Parts of the city are just being abandoned and ignored.

When the rioting was actually beginning to happen I would

hear white people say, "Oh, I'm getting out of town. I'm going to stay with family." They were literally separating themselves from the city. People say the same things: "Crime and schools, crime and schools," so therefore leave. If you do that, you're condemning the problems and they'll only get worse.

I grew up in the South and Baltimore is one of the most segregated places I've ever seen despite having Black leadership—having a Black mayor, a Black police commissioner and state's attorney. There's still a huge amount of segregation and pushing money to a few selected areas of the city. It's so much of a class thing. The community feels Stephanie Rawlings-Blake [the current mayor of Baltimore City] is very out of touch.

I was talking to the Crips and the Bloods [rival gangs who called a truce during the Baltimore riots] and they told me they were totally behind Sheila Dixon because they knew she grew up in Edmondson Village [a rough part of town]. They said: "She feels our struggle. She would come out and talk to us and she wouldn't bring a security guard because we love her and nothing would happen to her." But Stephanie Rawlings-Blake would never come out without a TV camera, security and an entourage. The community feels she doesn't listen to them and she doesn't talk to them, so within talks about race, there's also a huge class-divide within the Black community in Baltimore. Areas like Sandtown-Winchester, where Freddie Gray was arrested, are really ignored by a large portion of the city's political class.

I think the good thing that came out of the uprisings and what has happened over the last few weeks is that the poor and Black community has really had a chance to speak up on a level that has not happened in Baltimore before.

**Solution:** I think the solution is to invest, not to flee.

## Porter Ray, Rapper Recording Artist, Seattle, WA

I grew up in Capitol Hill, the central district of Seattle, where it seems to me like there's been the most gentrification taking place.

A lot of low-income housing has been torn down. New apartments and condos are being built and they're clearing low-income families out and moving them to south Seattle, making families leave homes they have been living in for most of their lives.

A lot of the Black businesses have shut down. There's no longer any Black restaurants, and many small and independent businesses are being shut down in the area as well. It's different now when I ride through my old neighborhood and I'm used to seeing a lot of African-American faces and that has changed. When kids get out of school now, I see a lot less Black children walking home from school. There are so many new faces. I've never been asked so many times, "Where are you from?" in my own city. That's not something I'm used to. Now there are a lot of implants and people that have migrated here. It's not as comfortable. I feel like a new face in my own neighborhood. It's a drastic change.

The tech and start-up companies are drawing a lot of people and the Seahawks are too. Seattle feels new and fresh to a lot of people, but it does seem like something that will completely remove African Americans from the city. [I think racism is a part of it as well] because that is how our system in this country has been built. There's an ingrained hatred for the African-American community.

I feel like it's something that's not going to stop. Maybe ten years from now, it's not going to be appealing for white people to live in the city and low-income families will be relocated back into the city. It's an everlasting cycle that I don't see stopping anytime soon.

**Solution:** I don't know what the solution would be. It's sad to say, but it's something we've gotten used to. I'm not even that old, so it's something that, in my lifetime, I've realized we've gotten used to, which is unfortunate. I think just talking about it and getting people to articulate a multitude of different stories can help bring a solution.

## Xavier Dphrepaulezz (Fantastic Negrito), Musician, Oakland, CA

My perspective on the East Bay is interesting because I grew up here in the '80s. Something happened then that set up all of this gentrification in my opinion. There was a war on the inner city in the '80s.

I had an experience where a kid I grew up with came to school with three thousand dollars. I had never seen three hundred dollars before and he said, "Man, they got this new shit called crack and people are going crazy." In one day it all changed and the American dream was finally attainable to us young Black men. It was fed to us that we were supposed to have cars, homes, money and power and we didn't know how to get it. There was never any money in the community, and then there it was. It changed the neighborhood forever and we're still living in the echoes of the crack epidemic.

We proceeded to seek out and destroy our own people. The people we targeted were about ten years older than we were and I always remembered that. To them, through all the frustration of the Black Panthers being destroyed and all of the progressive Black movements being decapitated, crack came and it felt good. They finally had something they could feel good about, and for us younger people we could finally afford cars and houses, and we did but we weakened and fractured our own community. I had to grow up and become an adult to realize this, because back then I was just a kid who wanted money and cars and to have the American dream, which is always on the backs of other people.

I feel like that is what set up gentrification, because it's natural for a predator to prey on the weak and disenfranchised and that's what is happening, it's easy now to just walk in and claim the neighborhood. The one thing that cannot be claimed is the culture. You cannot claim the culture because the culture came from struggle. But you can come in the neighborhood because the Bay Area is a beautiful place to live. Growing up here, it was one of the most diverse places.

My father used to tell me when I was growing up, "You never argue with someone with a gun," and I always thought, "Why is he always telling me this shit?" He'd say, "If the police stop you, you say, 'yes sir' and 'no sir,' never argue with anyone on the street with a gun. You completely comply and deal with them later, on a more level playing field." So, when the time came in the '80s when the police came and put us to the ground and put pistols to our heads, my father gave me the tools to deal with those situations. Back then, I didn't see so much of kids getting shot by police. I don't know the statistics, but somehow we knew how to deal with the police.

**Solution:** Men, however we can do it, let's start being men. Let's start taking responsibility for what we do. As Black men, we are all connected together. We need to get our shit together so we can get along with people better, so we can deal with women better. Here's what I have done: I have existed in collectives. We stopped thinking about the American dream and surrendered our money to each other. We said, "Whoever has a goal that's going to benefit all of us, we're going to support that 100%." Three years ago, I was playing on the streets and train stations and in east Oakland and downtown Oakland with a guitar. My collective supported me because they thought my music was an excellent project and they thought I was onto something. I was able to support my children and my family, so that's how we've done it. We have to solve this ourselves.

# Section One
# Music Reviews

I never professed to know very much, but there is something about hearing a sound and being able to paint a picture and a silhouette of a dramatic tale to surround a song, an album or a live performance that peaks the most dormant imagination.

I am an avid daydreamer, and when I listen to music my imagination goes into high gear, visualizing images and stories, and sometimes I even guess how the musician physically composed the song with zero information about the recording process. The trick to being accurate is doing it over and over and over again.

The trick to writing a good album review or a live review is that I allow my analytical mind to sit in the backseat of the Cadillac of my fantasies. You? You sit in the passenger side. The day I lose my ability to dream will be the day I drop you off on the side of the road in the hot sun and I speed off with arrogance and haste believing the music is about me. My radio will turn into 80 minutes of commercials and 10 minutes of 1:30 radio edits and I'll sit in my decaying Caddy smug and satisfied.

I do my best to listen to and review art.

*Arranged alphabetically by artist*

# Alice Coltrane, *Transfiguration* (Live, 1976)

It's been noted that 1976's *Transfiguration* is a culmination, and a sort of completion, of the body of work Alice Coltrane had been building since 1967. The title track from the eponymous live album (not released until 1978) was purposely titled to mark the beginning of Coltrane's spiritual-based compositional phase where she strictly composed Hindu-inspired chants and meditation music. Strong and entrancing, "Transfiguration" is perhaps most importantly a free jazz piece that contains absolutely no bells and whistles, and no Hare Krishna title or lyrics. It's just Coltrane on piano and organ, Reggie Workman on bass and Roy Haynes on drums, giving the audience at UCLA in Los Angeles an opportunity to hear what Coltrane was naturally working with.

This subtly bold expression of the transition of Coltrane's musical identity and composition style allows a last taste, or rather a sending-off from her traditional experimental and improvisational genius, into a more transcendental composi-tional style. *Transfiguration* is her leaving a satisfying musical remnant of a season of art that was never to be duplicated again, since the definition of transfiguration is complete change of form or appearance into a more beautiful or spiritual state. This one is for the enthusiasts who don't want chocolate in their peanut butter. It's as if she respectfully left something for the people who she knew would not spiritually ascend into the clouds with her. She knew that it was end of the road for her and some of her loyal, purist followers, and she did a brilliant job of jamming her heart out and, in the process, creating a flawless piece of work.

*Published: Aquarium Drunkard, April 2013*

# Blaze Foley, *Cold Cold World* (2013)

"Blaze is one of the most spiritual cats I've ever met; an ace finger picker; a writer who never shirks the truth."
—Townes Van Zandt

Blaze Foley was a bright shining star in the world of dark emotive country and folk music in the 1970s and '80s, before being gunned down in a murderous quip between a father and son, Concho and Carey January, on February 1, 1989. 24 years after his untimely death, a full-length album of songs from Blaze and his band, the Beaver Valley Boys, will be released next month via the San Francisco-based Secret Sevens Records/Lost Art Records. Entitled *Cold Cold World*, the album is a collection of recordings captured between 1979 and 1980 in a Texas studio that finds Foley and his band in top form. The title cut alone is a striking and profoundly well-mastered track that highlights Foley's genius and natural knack for writing simplistically calm, yet philosophical country ballads. *Cold Cold World* is an honest, reverent homage to a songwriter whose relevance should never be lost on this world.

*Published: Aquarium Drunkard, June 2013*

# Earl Sweatshirt, *Doris* (2013)

Nineteen-year-old hip-hop artist Earl Sweatshirt's full-length album, *Doris*, can be considered a post-modern feat and has the tendency at times to overshadow the innovative work of his counterpart, Odd Future-founder Tyler, The Creator. The stealthy, laid-back beats and rhymes of *Doris* are quietly reminiscent of the chopped-and-screwed era from Austin, Texas, but this young rapper's wisdom and self-awareness is truly the quality that stands at the forefront of his latest release.

There is a deep level of emotional intelligence and acknowledgment in this album, particularly in the second track, "Burgundy." He raps candidly about his family and his experience working to complete his album and the balance it took to create and release *Doris*.

"Burgundy" moves seamlessly into the fourth track, "Sunday," which is a revealing and surprisingly mature love song. Another heart-wrenching track on the album is "Chum," wherein Sweatshirt speaks about his return from exile at a boarding school in Samoa, where his mother sent him for behavioral problems right after he obtained viable attention and music industry acclaim for his first mixtape, *Earl*. "Hoarse" sports dark guitar riffs and seething musical rhymes that truly express Sweatshirt's ability to merge vocally and lyrically with any type of beat he his presented with.

*Doris* is elegantly disturbing as Sweatshirt continuously delivers real style and form without ever falling off a beat or straying away from each track's distinct subject matter. He has the rare ability to get an idea, feeling or general experience across in his songs and has a very unique tone to his style and delivery.

Sweatshirt's difficult experiences and his relationship with the music industry make *Doris* an album with uncannily dark and strained lyrics. Nonetheless, his delivery is authentic and creative, as is his expression of the irony of life's situations. The album draws you in more and more with its sensual and gritty beats and the well-thought-out flow from song to song. There isn't a song that sounds out of place on the track list.

*Doris* features a plethora of notable guests, including RZA, Frank Ocean and Tyler, The Creator, among others. Every artist delivers on *Doris*. It's incredible to hear the quality and depth of this very young lyricist. His heart and mind are very tied into his work, and it's been a really long time since the rap game has seen a true artist who pours so much depth and understanding into his music while almost completely avoiding cliché, shallow lyrics about getting money and being with women.

*Published: New York Amsterdam News, October 2013*

# Gary Wilson, *Feel the Beat* (2012)

Buy if you like: Frank Zappa, Beck

Gary Wilson may be the best rock comeback story of the millennium. Since his return to music after 20 years of inactivity, he hasn't wasted time recording new material. With *Feel the Beat*, Wilson continues his experimental pop/jazz journey, accompanied by long walks in the dark with his recurring mystery lovers, Linda and Cindy. The composer of "6.4 = Make Out" also sings about makeout sessions with new ladies and, on "Lugene Kissed Gary Last Night," someone whose gender is unknown and whose advances are apparently unwanted by the kiss-centric artist. The compositions and execution tend to be more sophisticated than on previous recordings, suggesting Wilson put a lot of time and thought into this album. Fun, whimsical and bound to encourage spontaneous dance moves, *Feel the Beat* is a worthy addition to Wilson's unconventional legacy.

*Published: Colorado Springs Independent, May 2012*

# J. Mascis at The Independent:
# Live Review (2014)

Dinosaur Jr. frontman J. Mascis was back in San Francisco on Saturday with his latest collection of solo, acoustic songs for a sold-out concert at the Independent [Nov 15].

Mascis arrived at the Independent around 9:30 pm, walking right through the crowd while the Australian folk duo Lulac finished their opening set. No one seemed to notice his pace as he made his way to the backstage entrance, and he was left unbothered.

Mascis' labelmates Luluc have been traveling on tour with him and played a lovely electro-acoustic set of sensuous indie-folk songs. Zoë Randell's voice was entrenched in a deep alto tone that was peaceful and mesmerizing. Their stage banter was endearing and the crowd politely applauded the band with disciplined adoration.

Luluc were off-stage for barely 15 minutes before Mascis sat down with his guitar. Promoting his new album, *Tied to a Star*, he played the single "Every Morning" and other cuts from the new release. His solo performances are interesting because he sits in front of a pedal board and seamlessly plays the melodies and leads of all the songs breaking from the acoustic folk and pop foundations for fuzzed-out riffs and bridges between songs.

Mascis also broke into songs from older Dinosaur Jr. albums, including "Where You Been." The crowd didn't seem to be as moved by Mascis' much-publicized cover of Mazzy Star's "Fade Into You," but his voice was magical and the performance was given with sincerity.

The show was simple, peaceful and moved at a pace that Mascis solely commanded. It was definitely minimal, but the crowd seemed engaged throughout—helped in part by fluid guitar solos that lasted sometimes more than 5 minutes, and his signature vocal style.

*Published: SF Station, November 2014*

# Kendrick Lamar, *To Pimp a Butterfly* (2015)

The highly anticipated album from rapper Kendrick Lamar was released March 16 and quickly became one of the most successful digital releases in history. *To Pimp a Butterfly* is Lamar's triumphant third studio album and has been met with rave reviews for its piercingly honest and Afro-centric subject matter.

With musical and lyrical cameos from George Clinton, Snoop Dogg, Ronald Isely and Bilal and public endorsements of praise from seasoned hip-hop artists such as Talib Kweli, Flying Lotus and Kanye West, *To Pimp a Butterfly* received record-breaking numbers on the digital-music-streaming program Spotify, racking up a staggering 9.6 million plays on the first day of the album's release.

This album holds nothing back. With singles like "I" and "The Blacker the Berry," Lamar opens up about his perspective and experiences as a Black man in America, his experimentation with psychedelic drugs and the evolution of his relationship with himself. *To Pimp a Butterfly* is a bold, expressive piece of music, and the media and music industry have not offered a negative peep about the album, despite its raw, fearless exploration of American race relations.

Elements of Afro-futurism, jazz and psychedelic music are all mixed in with the album's powerful beats. Lamar often delivers soliloquies of spoken word, storytelling and personal commentary throughout the album, giving the album variation and depth. The record was clearly thought out and crafted with very close attention to detail, making its artistic elements still seem effortless.

*To Pimp a Butterfly* could very well be considered one of the most important hip-hop albums to date. Lamar comes off as a visionary and sets the bar at a level that is not too high to reach but creates a new realm of art-nouveau hip-hop that will keep new generations of rappers looking deeply into themselves to achieve.

Lamar ends his album by seamlessly pasting together an interview-like conversation with the rapper Tupac Shakur in the song "Mortal Man." The album ends with humility as the young rapper asks Tupac about his perspective, as if he is hoping for advice on how to survive on his own as a natural leader and excellent lyricist.

*Published: New York Amsterdam News, March 2015*

# Pink Mountaintops at The Chapel: Live Review (2014)

The Pink Mountaintops performed last night [May 31] at The Chapel in the Mission District to a loyal crowd of friends and fans, who patiently waited for McBean and his new line-up—which includes Dead Meadow's Steven Kille, Will Scott, and Gregg Foreman of Cat Power—to take the stage.

McBean strolled through the venue with a peaceful flow in his step, but the night was colored by a dark undertone, thanks to a number of quiet quips that from McBean that mounted into a surprisingly violent climax at the show's end.

"I don't know, maybe it's just that weird thing of life and pushing through it, the beauty of it, the sadness and the happiness of it," McBean had said of his new album, *Get Back*, while he slowly sipped his first cocktail at the bar a few hours earlier. "The more you're on the planet, the more amazing things will happen to you, and the more terrible things will happen to you, and you have to have the ability to constantly shake it off."

While the hazy, eerie atmosphere coated the venue, LA's Giant Drag was able to play a sensually dark set of songs, completely appropriate for the early evening. The crowd slowly trickled in throughout the night, not quite filling the room, and people seemed to shift and cycle through the venue, never standing in one place for too long. There was never a moment where there was a complete loss of the crowd's attention, but there was a quiet level of distraction going on. Whether it was because everyone had a chance to drink as much as they could possibly consume by the time Pink Mountaintops stepped onto the stage or whether the band's hazy wall of sound was slightly lost in translation was not really clear. ("Me and Kille are the drunks and Gregg and Will are the sober guys," McBean had noted earlier.)

After opening with "How Can We Get Free?" and a fresh

song, "Ambulance City," from the new album, Stephen McBean broke a string and took his time to service and tune his guitar while the rest of the lineup improvised a song. Steve Kille swayed back and forth across the stage with his signature dance that closely resembles a confident swagger. After McBean got his guitar back in order, the set became more coherent and solid. The band flowed through "Wheels," "Plastic Man You're the Devil," and "The Second Summer of Love" and the crowd began settling in, planting their feet on the The Chapel's floor, finally beginning to engage with the music they were hearing.

Gregg Foreman, who has played with McBean as a duo and the sparsest version on Pink Mountaintops, shined. His erratically blissful guitar playing sewed the rest of the band's slightly eclectic instrumentation styles together. Kille and drummer, Steve Scott, are very different musicians. If not for Forman's unique experimental-psych guitar style, the band would have lacked an off-kilter characteristic that kept the crowd's attention during the middle and end of the show.

Everything seemed to flow peacefully as the show ended with the songs "New Teenage Mutilation," "Sweet 69" and "The Last Dance." McBean played solo for the last song, and it was endearing and really lovely to watch—until McBean suddenly smashed his guitar over his amp, hurling it over his head several times until it cracked, ending the show on a strangely violent note.

The band had joined him on stage seconds before McBean attacked his guitar, and they put their instruments down just as quickly as they had picked them up after McBean walked past them leaving the stage. The rest of Pink Mountaintops mingled with the crowd, seeming unaffected by McBean's behavior, allowing their non-inner circle to slowly disperse from the evening's odd occurrence. The show was weird, but the band is great.

*Published: San Francisco Bay Guardian, May 2014*

# Psychic Jiu-Jitsu, *Psychic Jiu-Jitsu* (LP, 2015)

The nouveau psych-rock band Psychic Jiu-Jitsu have released their debut full-length, self-titled album. The thing about Psychic Jiu-Jitsu is that they don't fit anywhere near a "genre check box" where you can neatly explain and entertain yourself with a number of comparisons to bands of the past, present or future. The album is refreshingly "out there," kicking the ten-track collection of songs off with the female-vocal-infused opening track, "Yulia's Capture at the English Front," starring the band's long-time friend and muse, Yulia Gorman. The next track, "Dreamachine," is another oldie-but-goodie deriving from early jams and recordings, becoming sketched out and perfected by a number of live performances of the song.

If you're looking for a friendly rock record in this album, you're not going to find it. The next songs, "Berlin Space Party," "World of Warldorf" and "Don't Bore Us," are unapologetic, youthful, fast-paced and experimental. Anyone who doesn't have a sense of humor, a love of experimental music and/or a young spirit won't get these songs and will never make it through the entire album. You'll get a pastiche of musical styles with the second cluster of songs, as "Slow Ringing in My Dreams" is a funk-infused track while "Golden Hair of the Sweet Sea Heir" is a whimsical country/ folk-influenced song that moves right into the space-ambient-sounding song, "Something Glistens." "Otto Vom" is the ninth song of the album and is appropriately (sort of appropriately) nine seconds long. The final song, "Black Marketeers of WWIII," is a post-apocalyptic track ending the album with an almost eight-minute ode to futuristic doom. You'll either like the *Psychic Jiu-Jitsu* album or you won't. It's not wise to make a chore out of listening to the album, but you should go into it with the determination to venture into uncharted psych-noise territory. This is a good debut effort from the band. If they choose to record another album, you should listen to that too, just to see how far-out they plan to get over time.

*Published: The Deli Magazine San Francisco, April 2015*

# Rowland S. Howard and Lydia Lunch, "Some Velvet Morning" (Rare, 1982)

Lee Hazlewood and Nancy Sinatra's "Some Velvet Morning." The coupling of a psychedelic country-rock pioneer and a struggling pop princess of the '60s. A risky, experimental and dubious piece of work that did, in fact, reach number 26 on the Billboard pop charts in 1968. It has since been covered just short of 20 times from 1968–2010, including this No Wave version, performed by Rowland S. Howard and Lydia Lunch. Released by 4AD in 1982, the duo's experimental and off-kilter take opened up new avenues of interpretation, adding a bit of humor to an '80s post-rock canvas, coming across more post-modern art project than pop song. On display: keyboardist Genevieve McGuckin's signature experimental piano aesthetics, Lydia's, well, Lydia-like vocals, Mick Harvey and, of course, one Rowland S. Howard.

*Published: Aquarium Drunkard, July 2013*

# Shabazz Palaces, *Lese Majesty* (2014)

You may remember experimental hip-hop artist extraordinaire Ishmael Butler from the New York-based, jazz-infused hip-hop trio Digable Planets from the early 1990s. He rapped under the moniker Butterfly, and almost two decades later he has re-emerged triumphantly as a part of the brilliantly unique intergalactic hip-hop collective Shabazz Palaces.

Butler and musical counterpart's Tendai Maraire's new album, *Lese Majesty*, is a spiritually potent collection of tracks that is so different from the mainstream's norm, it seems that he has set out to challenge and even redefine the definition of rap music of this era. With mature rappers rising in the realms of education, art and technology, it's a perfect time for *Lese Majesty* to emerge from the roots of this current African-American moment of commercial enlightenment.

The opening track, "Dawn of Luxor," opens the album in true "intro" form: slowly and quietly, softly driving you deeply into Shabazz Palaces' embellished aural realm. The first word of the album is "focus," urging you to lay back and pay attention to what the music has to offer throughout the remaining 17 tracks.

The next track, "Forerunner Forey," flows like a Flying Lotus track taken to the next level, with lush, artistic soundscapes and psychedelic ebbs and flows throughout the song. Butler never loses the beat and never misses a step as the music moves and swirls around his solid vocal flow.

The album moves forward with the songs, keeping close to home with a musical aesthetic that is almost ambient until you get to the seventh track, "The Ballad of Lt. Maj. Winnings." The song showboats purposely off-syncopated beats that could be considered out of place but should probably be thought of as an artistic evolution—or just a splash of color to ensure the album isn't redundant. Nonetheless, if the album continued to explore washed-out background sounds throughout the entire album, it would be acceptable and beautiful because Shabazz Palaces' confidence and proficiency is so above the bar and ahead of its time, it's just refreshing to know their work exists.

The album just gets weirder, particularly when you fall into the sonic world of the ninth track, "Ishmael." His bodacious ode to himself is very satisfying, as you get to listen to him struggle with his own fame, ego and spiritual reality. It is a common theme in his songs, and it is a pleasure to hear him speak with such honesty about a path he feels he has been chosen to embark upon. These explorations make his rhymes genuine and sensual.

*Lese Majesty* dips back into a watery, psychedelic compositional style with its fourteenth track, "Suspicion of Shape." The music expresses a shapeless vibe, giving way to wide-open strokes of sound and Butler's voice meshed with experimental noise echoing behind him.

The final track of the album, "Sonic Mythhap for the Trip," gives its listeners a clue that mind-altering drugs may be used to enjoy the album. It's clear from the moment the music begins that the record is a bit shamanistic. Butler has an enlightened perspective and searches for spiritual awakening, and he touches on many subjects of spirituality and living the human experience.

*Lese Majesty* is a strange record. Not everyone is going to understand it, but Butler's past work with Digable Planets has made it easy to move forward with him. His voice and face are recognizable; you can tell that he has not changed, he has just matured as an artist, and that fact is very comforting.

This album is a true piece of art. It grabs from the outer-space stylings of Afrika Bambaataa and Sun Ra. Shabazz Palaces is a true testament to the fact that hip-hop is going somewhere—it is elevating and becoming aware that there is more to life than what meets the eye.

*Published: New York Amsterdam News, August 2014*

# Spiritualized, *Sweet Heart Sweet Light* (2011)

File next to: Spacemen 3, My Bloody Valentine

Spiritualized's new album is a testament to leader Jason Pierce's uncanny ability to create consistently excellent records over the course of his British band's 22-year history. The album opens with "Hey Jane," an epic-length satirical counterpart to the Beatles' "Hey Jude" with an unexpectedly fatal conclusion— or maybe it's really just Pierce wondering why Jane isn't dead after nine minutes of him worshiping and brooding over her. While the album's first half candidly conveys the artist's experiences of lost love, the second is more in line with Pierce's gospel-soul ballad approach. ("Jesus won't you be my radio / Broadcast directions and tell me where I got to go.") It would be easy to criticize *Sweet Heart Sweet Light* for being almost a carbon copy of Pierce's previous work, but that would overlook just how brilliantly stylized and well-executed the album is. And these days, those qualities are hard to come by.

*Published: Colorado Springs Independent, December 2011*

# The Brian Jonestown Massacre at The Fox Theater: Live Review (2014)

Legendary Bay Area psychedelic band The Brian Jonestown Massacre played to a packed house at The Fox Theater in Oakland last night [May 8]. The band—led by singer Anton Newcombe and including founding members Matt Hollywood (guitar) and Ricky Maymi (guitar), along with long-time members Joel Gion (tambourine), Dan Allaire (drums), Rob Campanella (keyboard and guitar), Frankie "Teardrop" Emerson (guitar) and Collin Hegna (bass)—played songs from throughout its 26-year career, as well as new songs off its forthcoming album, *Revelation*, which is due for release on May 19.

The eight members were calm and professional as they walked onto the festively lit stage of the Fox. Anton greeted the audience by asking "How's everybody doing tonight?" and the crowd responded adoringly. The band kicked off the evening with "Whoever You Are" from its sixth album, *Give It Back*.

Early in the show, BJM performed a brand new song, "What You Isn't," which blended well with the band's older, classic songs that followed, including "Jennifer" and "I Got My Eye On You." The band only played a couple songs from its less-popular albums, and it entirely skipped the albums *My Bloody Underground*, *Who Killed Sgt. Pepper?* and *Aufheben*. The band's original material was augmented with a cover of Bobby Jameson's 1965 anti-war ballad "There's a War Going On."

Despite a couple of audio technical difficulties, the show went smoothly, and the notoriously agitated Newcombe showed no signs of drama (except during a brief exchange when he told Hollywood, who was talking to his bandmates between songs, that he'd prefer not to chat during the show). Overall, the band created an enthralling experience and played songs in a heartfelt manner, occasionally creating walls of sound that were euphoric.

Newcombe's voice sounded healthy, as he hit every note and projected seemingly without effort. Every moment felt like a priceless gift.

*Published: East Bay Express, May 2014*

# Section Two
# Columns

Revealing the secret of writing and maintaining a long-lasting column is beyond me. None of my columns or series have lasted longer than a few months, but that's ok. When I scrape them all together they still show signs of a cognitive stretch of ideas that exists very much so in my mind... just not on blogs. Such is life.

To write a column you have to have some messed-up experiences and learn from them. Being a broke-ass writer and having some insight on sex and dating is just a screwed-up manifestation of having the realization in retrospect of the things I've done wrong. I think though, more in regards to dating, that there is a sort of an intrinsic level of empathy that I possess. I've watched people fall in love and break up from when I was a very young girl. As a child, I could see what went wrong from the outside looking in and took mental notes of what not to do when I got older.

At this point in my life, I am single, but I can truly say I am safely independent and enjoy handsome suitors in a manner where I feel all is not lost.

If you want to write a column, live life and listen more than you speak. Watch more than you illustrate and make sure you keep your potential reader in mind at all times... If not, you'll just be writing *Bridget Jones' Diary*... Wait, that went on to make a bizillion dollars... Carry on then, I guess.

*Arranged alphabetically by column*

# How to Survive as a Broke-Ass Writer: Couch and Hostel Surfing

So, I've been on the road as a writer and musician for a little over a decade. The first time I officially became homeless I was 19 years old, and the first time I ran away from home was at age 15. I have always been a transient person. Working and moving has been my life, and I chose a career that allows me to travel often. As a journalist, I've flown from coast to coast to get interviews and exclusive tours of studios by my favorite artists.

Nonetheless, traveling, subletting, and couch and hostel surfing is not easy. Finding a place to rest your head every night can be a challenge when you're living from freelance check to freelance check. Now that I am almost 30, I have the financial means to negotiate costs for room and board and sublets.

Don't get me wrong, if you're making less than $1,000 a month, this article is not for you. This article is for broke-ass writers who work, receive wages for what they do and have wiggle room to get around and find temporary living situations that enable them to do their jobs well.

## Don't compromise—Skip the ghetto

Just because you don't have a lot of money, it doesn't automatically mean you have to live in a bad neighborhood. I am from west Baltimore, MD, and if you're like me, you don't ever want to spend your adulthood in a place that you did not enjoy very much when you were a child. Find cute towns on the outskirts of the city that are a train ride away. A commute may be a little annoying but your safety and comfort should be a top priority. You cannot write well if you're not in a peaceful place.

## For a fast move-in—Airbnb not Craigslist

Craigslist is great for permanent housing and rooms, but if you

ONLY have $1,000, which is not enough to pay first and last month's rent to move in, Airbnb is a great alternative. It's a little pricey, but you can reserve a place for 30 days for $900–$1200 (sometimes less if you get lucky) and you won't have to pay a deposit. If you get along with your renters during the first month at your Airbnb room, you can negotiate with them personally and maybe keep your place longer.

## Hostels—Choose hippie over chic

Choose a nice down-to-earth hostel over the swanky alternatives that are usually located downtown or in central areas. If you like being surrounded by ultra-rich Euro and Asian people in their early twenties, that's fine, but a nice cozy bed-and-breakfast-style hostel will allow you to be more incognito, and the rates will be much lower. Being a successful hostel and couch surfer is about being personable and working and living with renters who can understand you on a human level. If they see you as just another dollar, you will be expendable, and could lose the little stability you hoped for while being there.

## Have a positive attitude

If you think you can stay at your friends' and family's houses while you are a negative brooding person, you've got it very twisted. No one wants to be around a complainer. Have a bright attitude, and offer to pick up small expenses you can afford. Buy a bottle of wine, cigarettes for smokers, offer to pick up groceries. Be funny and positive. Be a joy to be around.

## Make your presence scarce

Even if you're a freelancer, don't sit around on the couch every day, or even at the kitchen table on your laptop for 18 hours a day. Go to coffee shops, take the time to explore the city and work in different spaces. Come back around at 8 or 9 pm. You want people you're staying with to have space. If you're around all the time, they will begin to see faults and idiosyncrasies in your behavior. I'm not saying you'll be judged, but people do tend to pay attention to "unstable" people to try and figure out why they don't have their shit together. Be aware, be functional and mature. Most importantly, be as independent as you can.

## Line things up 2–3 weeks in advance

If you know you have enough money for a hostel for two weeks, make sure you're lining up your next place immediately. Know where your finances are coming from for the month. Let your friends and family know you may need to stay with him a few weeks down the line. They will be more prepared, and it gives people a chance to help out and make accommodations for you.

## Be an adult

If you're crashing somewhere, don't sleep until noon. Get up in the morning, shower, have money for your own food, weed or whatever you do. Conduct yourself in a responsible manner. You're a professional writer; you're a respected journalist, critic, author or blogger. Match the respect you have in your career in your personal life. People will want to invest in you more when they see you working, writing and handling business.

*Published: Broke-Ass Stuart, August 2014*

# How to Survive as a Broke-Ass Writer: Using Your Domestic Awesomeness for Cool Side Jobs

There are grown people in this world who don't know how to separate colors when washing clothes. There are people who cannot hand-wash dishes without leaving food caked on the edges of plates and glasses.

As a broke-ass writer and avid traveler, I started realizing that my domestic skills could be a big help in allowing me to support myself. Whether I was dog- and apartment-sitting in Central Park West in New York City or being able to cook a wonderful hearty meal for my rock-and-roll male housemates in Baltimore and San Francisco, I have been able to be a loving and useful friend, domestic goddess and confidant for a number of people over the years.

What do you have to offer, particularly when you are trying to make it in a major city on a writer's pay?

Learning domestic skills will offer you a place in a field that is flexible and will never run short of opportunities.

## Dishes

Dishes are the number one most annoying chore in the Universe. It is a meticulous job, and even if you have a dishwasher, everything has to be sorted one by one.

Buy your own soap. It's always cool to have dishwashing, laundry and shower soap on-hand so you're not using other people's toiletries and cleaning supplies. It can be a little expensive, but it is an expense that will help you avoid conflict.

## Scrub

Scour, then wash. Even if you don't see gunky food on plates, make sure you scour dishes (obviously not crystal or certain glass dishes) with that rough green side of the sponge first.

Line things up on the drying rack by size and by the type of dish. It makes your dishwashing look organized and intentional.

## Wash silverware and the sink

Don't try to avoid washing silverware. Also, wash the sink when you are done. I know this all seems really silly, but it makes a huge difference when it comes to completing a job to where it is satisfactory to a discerning eye.

## Counters and surfaces

Be mindful of how kitchen and sink counters are left. If you brush your teeth or wash your face and drench the entire bathroom counter, someone is going to come in and lay their clean clothes down before a shower, only to have them become soaked (it happens to me all the time, and I can't stand it). It makes people really angry.

After you cook in the kitchen or use the sink in the bathroom, make sure you clean and dry counter and sink surfaces.

## Laundry

Washing towels is a great skill to have. Keeping the bathroom loaded with clean towels and washcloths is so helpful. No one wants to jump out of the shower to find there are no clean or dry towels anywhere! It just makes life so much more comfortable. Make sure when you fold the towels they are all facing the same way when put away in the closet. You want everything to be stacked and looking great.

Separating clothes by color in the wash is crazy important! If you think you can throw a red sweater in the washer with a bunch of white towels, you are totally wrong. Wash whites with other light-colored clothes, make sure dark-colored clothes are washed together, and fabrics that are bright-colored should be washed together.

## Beds

Make your bed and change your drooley pillow cases often. Enough said. Learning how to make a bed takes practice. Just make sure the sheets and comforters don't have major wrinkles and everything is tucked in and looking crisp. Have high expectations for yourself and high standards for your bed. You know what a beautifully made sleeping area looks like. Push yourself until you know how to make your space and others' sleeping areas pristine.

## Animal-sitting

Animal-sitting has to be the most lucrative domestic skill you can have. Being able to connect with, walk, clean up after, play with and maintain a relationship with other people's pets can bring you a lifetime of paid animal-sitting gigs, and usually very nice temporary roofs over your head.

Taking care of animals is not really something that can be taught. Making sure their food and water dishes are full is one thing, but being able to communicate and having an animal obey you and want to spend time with you is another thing. If you genuinely don't like animals, don't fake it, and if you have allergies, don't send yourself to the hospital just to tack on another hustle.

You've got to be pretty emotionally open to take care of pets. Make sure you are there for them and not just for the money or the nice digs.

Be sure to ask your clients for referrals!

## Baby-sitting

Kids are loud and sticky, but if you have the patience to take care of them you will be able to supplement some income while you are work on your writing career. If the child or children are under a year old, you can count on them sleeping all the time, and you'll only have to make sure they are clean, dry, fed and comfortable.

If the children are older, you're going to need a lot of patience and the ability to connect with very young, dynamic personalities. Your communication skills and emotional intelligence have to be strong, because during one gig you could be sitting a shy quiet child, and the next weekend you could be watching an intense extrovert. Nanny or "manny" skills are incredibly useful.

*Published: Broke-Ass Stuart, September 2014*

# How to Survive as a Broke-Ass Writer: Dating and Relating

If you're a writer, it probably means you're a moody introspective introverted dork. I mean that in the kindest and most affectionate of ways, because I am one of you. Being a successful writer means you've probably learned the art of charm and can connect with pretty much anyone on the planet for a certain amount of time, but how do you survive after you really get to know a person and you begin to see their flaws, and they've already passive-aggressively called you out on a few of yours?

Your job is to be an informer or an entertainer. You're an artist, but does that make you a likeable and relatable human being? This week, I thought I'd give you some tips on how to relate to people on a genuine level. I have recently learned how to balance friendships and family relationships and even a close relationship with someone of the opposite sex without any dramatic meltdowns... Well, without disagreements that were not manageable and survivable.

Let's explore a few things I've learned along the way about getting along with people as a broke-ass writer:

## Accept that the solution starts with rooting out the problem — Self-awareness

It's more than just wanting to be able to relate to people and to attain stronger and less turbulent relationships — it is about being prepared to put in time to evaluate the root problems you are having with your own actions. Relationships are a two-way street.

Whether you book an appointment with a therapist or analyst, read a number of self-help books, or just sit down and think about what you've been doing over the last few years, congratulate yourself on taking the time to evaluate ownership of your problems. It is a hard pill to swallow. No one likes to admit that they need to change because they may have been going about things the wrong way, but that is a lesson in humility.

## Surround yourself with people who make good decisions

Look around at the people you spend the most time with. Do they make good decisions? Do they have similar goals, and most importantly, do they have the same values as you do? If you are a person who takes people's feelings into consideration and you make real efforts to make others feel comfortable by being loyal and reliable, do your friends reflect that behavior? Are your guy- or girlfriends sleeping with multiple lovers (and not in an honest polyamorous way), and trying to get over on commitments and responsibilities at every turn?

## Pay attention

If you take some time to look around and you find you are not really happy with the way your friends behave themselves, treat other people or treat themselves, you might want to make a plan to meet new friends.

## Find a guru... or a mentor

This stems from the process of surrounding yourself with people who make you feel like you can become a better person and a better "relater." Finding someone older than yourself, whom you admire, will give you a lot of insight you could never attain from even the wisest peer.

Having a mentor or an older platonic friend will give you an insider's look at life experiences and morals to valuable lessons.

Peep what Ram Dass has to say about it.

## Be kind, not "yourself"

When people say, "I'm being myself," it is usually a defensive response to someone criticizing their behavior. People don't want to be around someone who is angry or complaining all the time.

Life is hard, but the point of having friends is to be around people who can help you make enjoyable memories.

Be selective about what you share with people because something you say that could be "venting" to you, could turn others off completely.

## Build a little mystery

Being private and laid back can be sexy and it is definitely attractive. Give others a chance to learn about you slowly. If you give your whole life-story on the first play-date you will: a) come off long-winded and self-centered... and desperate for attention; and b) leave nothing to the imagination for the person to ponder when you separate from them.

Draw out your relationships. Patience is key. Be a puzzle they want to piece together for years on end.

## Don't have sex on the first meeting... or official date

This particular column is for relationships and friendships, but in this day and age 20- and 30-somethings and beyond are not "defining" their roles in relationships. If you're not going to live by traditional relational and gender roles, then I'm just going to say this to everyone:

Sleeping with someone on the first date or meeting will almost guarantee you will not get called back for another date. This theory has been tested by me personally and when I stopped sleeping with my lovers too early, I was able to obtain more fulfilling and long-lasting relationships with my partners.

## Have your personal morals and values carved out

If you're a Satanist, that's fine, but be willing to express your ideals and morals with confidence so others know where you're coming from. If you live in a grey area, you're going to attract people who are unsure of themselves as well. That makes for a messy, wishy-washy friendship/relationship.

## Let others help you

Let others contribute and invest in you. Millennium-women and feminists: want to make a new friend or partner run for the hills? Flip out on them for opening a door for you or wanting to pay the tab on your meal. Men, what to turn off a partner? Be overbearingly helpful by never letting them pay for dinner after you did 3 or 4 times.

## Let your partner give back

They will feel smothered by your kindness and will begin to feel like you are controlling if you don't. You know you certainly are not controlling, but opening up, putting your pride aside and allowing your partner to do the dishes, make the bed, pay the bill, open the car door for you, cook the meal, pay for the movie, choose the movie, etc. will create a give-and-take dynamic that is very healthy.

## Love yourself

Okay, we're writers so we're narcissists, right...? Well, yes, but not really. Just because we are confident about our books or articles being received well, it doesn't mean we as people believe we're going to be received well by others.

If you think others don't like you, it is probably because you don't like yourself.

Can you hang out with yourself? Do enjoy being alone? If you do, that is very healthy. If you find yourself always looking to connect with other people to avoid spending more than a few hours alone, then you should probably take some time and explore why you may be avoiding yourself.

Face your painful thoughts and memories and conquer them. You can do it! LOVE YOURSELF!

*Published: Broke-Ass Stuart, October 2014*

# How to Survive as a Broke-Ass Writer: What Editors Want

Before I became a professional editor and journalist, I was a super-green blogger trying to build an impressive portfolio. I have achieved all that I have because I had a few editors and writers in my life who were incredible mentors. Scott Schultz of *L.A. RECORD* and Thomas Murphy of the *Denver Westword* laid the groundwork for me to obtain a great work ethic and helped me learn the reality of what it takes to write a great story.

I currently work as the editor for *The Deli Magazine San Francisco* and am an entertainment reporter for the *New York Amsterdam News* among other publications. I keep it simple these days, but I've learned a lot along the way.

Of course, to this day I have to work to maintain great communication with my editors. I am not always perfect, but I know that being honest and ambitious can help any writer. I'm going to give some pointers on how to know what editors want and how to keep your job as a journalist and creative writer.

## Read and understand the publication you'd like to write for

Every publication has something called "a voice." The voice of a publication is a general verbal and grammatical flow that stays consistent through the entire issue. VICE focuses on immersion journalism and humor. If you're not into being sarcastic and a bit sadistic in your writing, don't submit your work to VICE. *The New York Review of Books* is a highly intellectual and opinionated publication. If you can't crack open your soul and eloquently write exactly what you think while making courageously sweeping statements about politics, society and anthropology, you might not want to submit to them.

Link your style and taste with the publications you plan to

write for... or vice versa.

## NEVER pitch to a writer

NEVER try to submit your work to a writer. First of all, they are your competition and you asking them for an "in" makes you look very unprofessional. Unless they are a close friend, no writer is ever going to give you their editor's email address because if you are a crappy writer, you will make them look bad, and if you are a great writer, you may surpass them quickly. Plain and simple. Only pitch and submit to editors.

## Quietly stalk your editors

*Don't be creepy.* I just mean there are ways to find editors' work emails without having to ask other people. First of all there is a "Contact Us" section at the bottom or top of every online magazine. If you can't find the editor's information there, look for a section on the menu called "About Us." You'll be able to find the editor's direct email.

LinkedIn is a great way to connect to editors. Twitter is a great way as well.

PS: PERSONAL FACEBOOK MESSAGES ARE NOT GOOD. Leave people alone unless you know they'll be cool... but still use that method wisely and sparingly.

## Read your editor's writing

Almost all editors are writers. You will rarely find an editor who did not start out as a journalist, author or blogger. Editors will most likely continue to write for their publication, so if you know their name read their work! When you pitch an idea, you can tell them how much of a fan you are and reference their articles. They love that. Really.

## So you stalked them and found their work email

You've been reading a publication for years, you've got a strong resume and samples and the editor's email. Now it's time to pitch. Be very clear in your subject line. Editors IGNORE 90% of emails. Write eye-catching pitches in your subject line and you'll get your pitch read.

Here are some examples of my pitch subject lines:

"Pitch: Guaranteed Publish—Interview with The Breeders"

"Live Review / Interview—Pink Mountaintops—May 28th The Chapel"

"Pitch/Sample Draft—Wash Post Style"

## Working with your editor

Your pitch has been accepted and you have the assignment. Nice work. Once you get the green light, leave your editor alone. There's nothing to say until a couple of days before the assignment is due. If you're reviewing a live event, just give a heads-up and confirm you're going to the show and ask if there's anything they need or want you to include in the piece. It's always good to send an "I'm alive and about to send you my article" email.

## After you submit your piece

Most of the time you're going to get notes on your submitted article. This means your editor is going to ask you to make a few or a million corrections on your piece. Don't get defensive. Be professional and make the changes. Don't make excuses.

You're a professional writer and an adult, so I'm not saying don't clarify or stand up for something if you think it should stay in your piece, but if you want to get another assignment, step lightly. You knew who you were writing for and the voice of the publication before you got the assignment, so do what you have to do to get published time and time again.

## Once you're published

They'll send you a link to the published online version of your piece. You can respond saying thank you and that you look forward to a great future with them. Don't contact your editor again unless you're going to pitch another piece. I mean, if you guys become friends and want to have cocktails like our awesome editor Stuart, by all means... but it doesn't usually work that way.

UNTIL NEXT TIME... keep writing, and do it well!

*Published: Broke-Ass Stuart, November 2014*

# How to Survive as a Broke-Ass Writer: Surviving Writer's Depression

There are a number of bright sides to being a writer, but I'll have to admit that there are probably more dark issues that writers face in their day-to-day lives and creative processes than we (writers) like to admit. A popular stigma is alcoholism (I personally have a coffee addiction but tomato-tom-ah-to) and we're looked upon as the most unrealistic and unmotivated artists in creative arts. That's why writers are rarely called artists when musicians, painters and sculptors can use the terms inter-changeably. Nonetheless, most of the unsavory generalized traits of writers can be managed with maturity and rather quickly; except for depression. If you ask any writer, I can put money on the fact that many of them will admit that they struggle with depression.

A few nights ago, I was in bed and slept for 14 hours. My kidney stones were blaring and I was experiencing the harsh realization that I was sleeping alone in bed again after a stint of sharing it with a partner—I was exhausted and became depressed. On top of all that, I had a few deadlines due the next morning. I thought to myself, "Well, I feel like shit. This is probably a good time to write about what to do when you're depressed as hell and have to make your living as a writer."

## When the depression comes on from illness

If you're one of those writers who is actually obsessed with being a writer and works on a number of projects, pieces or chapters at once, you probably don't notice when sickness begins to slowly cast its shadow upon your body. Your immune system has little ways of telling you something is wrong before full-blown symptoms occur. If you feel yourself get a slight headache, tight muscles or a foggy head, you might want to jump on taking some

Ibuprofen, Vitamin Water with B-6 and B-12 in it and get some extra rest. If you don't try to heal those small symptoms, you'll end up laid up in bed unable to move without having the slightest idea why.

Not knowing the cause of an illness or how to treat it can bring on depression. Being helpless and incapacitated can be frustrating for anyone. Take care of your body!

## If you are depressed and you have been diagnosed with depression by a psychiatrist

This is a bit of a tough subject because I am not a mental-health professional, but I think it is safe to say many writers have gotten to a point, particularly early on in their careers, where there needed to be some evaluation in regards to mental-health issues. I mean, if you have family members telling you you're crazy for wanting to take on a career that makes very little money and can't solidify a healthy future for yourself for years and years, it's easy to begin to believe them.

When people look down on you for "constantly scribbling in your notebook" or "being obsessed with your laptop" it can take a toll on your perception of yourself. Belittling environments and comments can get to you and make you wonder if you are a crackpot. It's really sad.

If you see a psychiatrist after going through the motions with a therapist, and you're told you suffer from depression, take the steps you need to take to get better. Medication is fine, because depression can be brought on by a chemical imbalance, but taking extra steps to making choices that make you feel COMFORTABLE in life will kill a lot of turmoil. Knowing it is going to be a long road and not idealizing this job, rejection and the effort it takes to succeed can ward off an emotional nose dive.

## If you're depressed due to a break-up

This is probably the most common and relatable situation that brings on a bout of depression. My advice? Write about it! Take your pain and your past and share it with the world... or just in a journal. I personally get inspired to write my columns by some real-life situations I go through. I am pretty raw from a separation from a guy and I think pitching a story idea and having it be accepted by my editor really helped me feel my ideas and emotions were valid. It also meant I could go ahead and help others through their problems.

This is not a relationship column so I'm just going to say that all the feelings of rejection, loss and pain really taper off over time. You'll be standing when the initial sting subsides... but as a writer, what are you going to do? Lose your job because some jerk left you?? You're better than that.

### If you're depressed and completely bedridden

Hopefully you have a laptop, because you should just write in bed. I mean, problem solved.

### If you're depressed and feel like you need to whine to everyone about it

If you have a career where the press actually cares about you, you should probably keep your dirty laundry to yourself. If you're happy just being a member or the press or an underground poet or author, remember that you're an adult and your family and friends have full lives as well.

If you refuse to write about it and blab about your problems all over town in an unstructured way, you may lose credibility by showing your weaknesses to people. I'm not paranoid—writers are thought-leaders and creative people. If you're expressing yourself in a manner that is a bit immature, people may stop reading your work. I know you're human, but you're also a grown up.

**If you're depressed and you've never been depressed, ever**
Then you're not depressed… so, just wait it out. Cry it out.
*Published: Broke-Ass Stuart, December 2014*

# The Nerve Sex Mixtape:
## A Soundtrack for First Times

The trick to a good sex mixtape is not in how many songs you can cram onto an mp3 playlist or CDR, but in finding the right collection of music that sets a mood. A great sex mixtape loosens sensual inhibitions and sexual reservations without being too overbearing.

If you're planning on sleeping with someone you're seeing for the first time, then look to a sex mixtape that will be non-invasive, sensual, and unlikely to offend your one-night stand's personal music taste. It's super important to avoid mainstream love songs with strong catchy hooks. Popular songs will abduct your sex partner's emotional attention from your lovemaking, and you'll find yourself pumping to the beat of Janet Jackson's "What Have You Done for Me Lately?" Sexual activity to up-tempo tracks or songs with strong beats can definitely be fun, but it can also turn your bed into a Cyndi Lauper dance-party. Let me put it to you straight: The '80s were not sexy, Lil' Wayne is not sensual, death metal is terrifying, and Britney Spears will leave you single and horny for the rest of your life. If you like to have sex to the music you blare in your car every morning, then you're never going to create a mixtape that's going to draw out a subtler type of intimacy.

When sleeping with a person for the first time, you likely won't know what kind of music they are into. Try to slip in a myriad of genres like psych-rock, soul, indie-rock, and an alternative mainstream song. Jazz is always a sexy touch for a first-time mixtape. It's a risky touch, but if you play Ornette Coleman for the right lover, you'll have them forever… or at least three times a week.

In the interest of improving your sex life, I've created the perfect mixtape for a first-time sensual encounter. Now you won't have to worry about any drama. These songs are simple, sexy, erotic and won't jar the bass in your speakers to the point that you forget what position you were attempting to twist your lover into. Enjoy the music and happy first-time sexing!

1. D'Angelo—How Does It Feel
2. Dead Meadow—At Her Open Door
3. Bilal—Soul Sista
4. Lana Del Rey—Blue Jeans
5. Nothing Even Matters—Lauryn Hill
6. Deerhunter—Helicopter
7. Bonnie Prince Billy—Lay And Love
8. Pink Floyd—Fearless
9. Allen Stone—The Wind
10. Ornette Coleman—Peace

*Published: Nerve.com, May 2013*

# The Nerve Sex Mixtape:
# How to Say You're Sorry

There are times in any couple's relationship when things get rocky. Whether it be about communication, money, sex, time, or family and friends, there are a plethora of circumstances that can create conflict and friction in people's romantic interactions.

When creating a mixtape that is going to convey a sense of regret after you've had a gnarly fight, you have to be seriously discerning about the songs you choose. Not all the songs have to be ballads and super sappy, but it's important that you choose tracks that are not too humorous or tongue-in-cheek. If your lover is already mad at you, it's not a great idea to try and bring humor to a situation they still may be sour about.

Letting your partner know that you yearn for their forgiveness, or their presence if they've left you, is one key to an "I'm sorry" mixtape. You want them to not only know that you're hurt about how things turned out, but that you want them to return to your life. If you continuously say you're sorry without saying, "Hey, come back to me," they'll get the message, but won't be as moved to take action to communicate with you.

Also, when you send the mixtape, give a few days before you ask for a response. This mixtape isn't meant to be pushy or invasive; it's meant to ease the pain of a prior intense confrontation.

Here are ten songs I've chosen as a way to musically represent your repentance. They'll let your scorned lover know that you really care, and that you want them to return to your life.

1. Frank Ocean—Thinking About You
2. Janet Jackson—I Get Lonely
3. Panda Bear—You Can Count On Me
4. Nico—These Days

5. LL Cool J—I Need Love
6. Etta James—I Just Want To Make Love To You
7. Sonic Youth—Bull In The Heather
8. The Brian Jonestown Massacre—Open Heart Surgery
9. The Roots feat. Erykah Badu—You Got Me
10. The Animals—Don't Let Me Be Misunderstood

*Published: Nerve.com, June 2013*

# Section Three
# Essays, Series and Profiles

I do my best to have saved up a well of emotional energy before I write an essay. I don't write them often because essays sit right on the edge of journalism and should be coveted for moments when you really have something to say. Any other time, it's best to work as a critic or a reporter so when you find a topic that moves you to express yourself, or experience something in your life that makes you want to tell the world, the significance isn't lost in the redundancy of your constant written declarations.

In one of my rare political pieces, I covered Assata Shukur. To be very honest, I'm not sure why I pitched the idea to my editors, but there was something about her life, and the fact that she became the first woman to be added to the America's Most Wanted list by the FBI, that jolted me to tell a bit of her story.

I wrote a couple of rare essays about my feelings and relationships, which anyone in my personal life knows I am very protective of. I have moments when I want to shine some light on the inner workings of my emotional life, but they probably only occur once every year or two. Who wants to be a "one-note" writer? Not me.

*Arranged alphabetically by publication*

# Why Feminists Should Care About the FBI's Hunt for Assata Shakur

Last week, the FBI named former Black Panther and member of the Black Liberation Army Assata Shakur as the first woman on its Most Wanted Terrorist list. This dubious milestone occurred 40 years to the day after she was, as she describes, unfairly convicted of shooting and murdering State Trooper Werner Foerster in New Jersey on May 2, 1973.

An all-white jury convicted Shakur of shooting the state trooper, who stopped her car for having a tail light out. Shakur was shot twice in the altercation—including once in the back—and there was evidence that her hands were raised in the air, but she received a sentence of life plus 33 years in prison, served two years in solitary confinement, then escaped. Forty years later, on May 2, 2013, the FBI and state of New Jersey have offered a $2 million reward for her capture.

The issue here is not whether Shakur committed the crime or not. That's impossible to know, given the racism of the justice system and the FBI at the time. Though the court felt she was guilty beyond a shadow of a doubt, in 1978 the National Conference of Black Lawyers and its allies sent a petition to the UN that noted Shakur's case was one of the worst examples of "a class of victims of FBI misconduct... who as political activists have been selectively targeted for provocation, false arrests, entrapment, fabrication of evidence, and spurious criminal prosecutions."

What we can know for certain is that her placement on the FBI's Most Wanted list this month shows that while the 1970s are behind us, the racial politics of the time continue to have an effect today.

Shakur (also known as Joanne Chesimard) has always maintained her innocence. After her escape from prison, she fled to Cuba and was granted political asylum. She remains there today, despite the FBI's attempt to extradite her back to the United States in 1998, when they asked the Pope to use a visit to Cuba to order her into the hands of the US government. In response to the state's letter to the Pope, Shakur wrote her own open letter to the Pope that explains her philosophy and innocence:

> *To make a long story short, I was captured in New Jersey in 1973, after being shot with both arms held in the air, and then shot again from the back, I was left on the ground to die, and when I did not, I was taken to a local hospital where I was threatened, beaten and tortured. In 1977, I was convicted in a trial that could only be described as a legal lynching. In 1979, I was able to escape with the aid of my fellow comrades. I saw this as a necessary step, not only because I was innocent of the charges against me, but because I knew that in the racist legal system of the United States, I would receive no justice. I was also afraid that I would be murdered in prison. I later arrived in Cuba where I am currently living in exile as a political refugee. The New Jersey State police, and other law enforcement officials, say they want to see me brought to justice, but I would like to know what they mean by justice.*

That is quite the contrast to the statement delivered by African-American male FBI agent Aaron Ford at the press conference on her addition to the FBI's Most Wanted list last week: "Joanne Chesimard is a domestic terrorist who murdered a law enforcement officer execution-style… We will not rest until this fugitive is brought to justice."

"Execution-style" is exactly the same phrase the FBI used when hunting for Shakur on a murder charge in 1972, when it also described her as the "revolutionary mother hen" of the Black Liberation Army. Now, she's not a "mother hen" but a "domestic terrorist."

So, we understand that Shakur has been targeted by men of her own race, who care nothing of her ethical fortitude or the pervasive racism that colored her arrest and trial, but instead demand that she be handled as a domestic terrorist and enemy of the United States of America.

Calling Assata Shakur, a powerful aid in the civil rights movement, a domestic terrorist is a scare tactic. She opposes a government that seems to aim to maintain oppressive control over American minorities and women. Shakur maintains her fight to protect and advocate for the freedom of diverse communities in American culture.

Shakur's prosecution in 1973 did not happen in a vacuum. Since 1967, the FBI was both secretly and overtly working to "neutralize" what they considered "black nationalist hate groups" like the Panthers. Shakur's case was one of many where Black activists were investigated, pilloried in the media, and prosecuted on questionable evidence.

Angela Davis, for example, was arrested and tried in 1970 for allegedly providing a gun that was used to kill Judge Harold Haley. Numerous groups and some big donors rallied to support her case, raising bail money, and funding a legal defense. After 18 months in jail, Davis was acquitted of all charges and set free.

Unlike Davis, who was a professor at UCLA, Shakur was relatively unknown before her trial. A jury deemed her guilty and she made the choice to live as a refugee. If Angela Davis had been found guilty for her crime, she and Shakur would have a lot more in common. Nonetheless, there is respect and solidarity between these two women. A conviction is the only thing that has deemed their fates to be perceived as night and day.

*Published: Bitch Magazine Online, May 2013*

# Fighting for the Right to Go Topless

This past week, the news broke that New York City began to instruct its police officers this winter to make sure they act accordingly to legality of women going topless in public. It's easy to dismiss this law with a punch line, but the truth is that instructing all of New York's police force to leave topless women alone is groundbreaking and part of a long-running movement led by women who have fought for topless equality.

New York's instructions to its officers likely came about as the result of the lawsuit filed by performance artist Holly Van Voast, who was arrested several times for going topless in public. From the *New York Times*:

> *The suit lists 10 episodes in 2011 and 2012 in which the police detained, arrested or issued summonses to Ms. Van Voast, 46, for baring her breasts at sites that included the Oyster Bar in Grand Central Terminal, in front of a Manhattan elementary school, on the A train and outside a Hooters restaurant in Midtown. The last episode, the suit says, ended with her being taken by the police to a nearby hospital for a psychiatric evaluation.*
>
> *Each complaint against her was dismissed or dropped, her lawyers said, for one simple reason: The state's highest court ruled more than two decades ago that baring one's chest in public — for noncommercial activity — is perfectly legal for a woman, as it is for a man.*

Van Voast isn't alone—plenty of folks believe that the right to bare their breasts is worth fighting for. Groups like Topfreedom and the nudist group Go Topless—who established the national "Go Topless Day" in 2007—have advocated for years that being able to go topless is a step forward for gender equality in the United States. They believe that women deserve the same treatment as men who are allowed to appear in public shirtless-as-they-please. We often take women's rights for granted, but legally, the United States has unabashedly described women's bodies as "lewd."

Topfreedom sells the idea of legal toplessness as simply an issue of equal rights. Their statement of mission reads:

> *Our basic claim is that women deserve equal rights. We do not suggest that women or men should go about with bare breasts. That is every individual's decision. We do believe that since men may choose to do so in many situations, women must also be able to at least in the same situations. Without penalty of any kind.*

That's what the New York police department is now enforcing: equality of toplessness. The New York policy change isn't coming out of the blue. Local jurisdictions have seen several key cases that have become staples in the legal battle between women, their breasts, and the law. People take getting naked seriously.

*Policymic* reports a specific and crucial case to the movement:

> *In the 1992 case People v. Ramona Santorelli and Mary Lou Schloss, the New York Court of Appeals ruled in favor of two women who were arrested with five others for exposing their breasts in a Rochester park, holding the law void as discriminatory. The ruling was put to the test in 2005, when Jill Coccaro bared her breasts on Delancey Street in New York, citing the 1992 decision, and was detained for twelve hours. She subsequently successfully sued the city for $29,000.*

In addition to New York, there are a few states who have overturned arrests and prosecution of women who have appeared in public without a top. Florida and Oregon share a similar law that protects female nudity as free speech. As long as a topless woman is protesting for a cause or making some sort of political statement with her body, she is protected by the First Amendment. In Oregon, several cases (including one where a man stripped at the airport to protest the TSA) have upheld the state law that nudity is only indecent exposure if its intent is to arouse. In Florida, a woman challenged anti-nudity laws and won in 2006 after she was arrested for going topless at a protest at Daytona Beach.

Meanwhile, all the way back in 1979, the Hawaii Supreme Court ruled that women can sunbathe in public without their tops as long as they are not committing "lewd acts." The rest of the country is just catching up.

I definitely applaud the city of New York for addressing the topless law with their local police force. This affords topless woman their rights and the protection of the police force, so that they can safely expose their bodies when it feels right to them. Yes!

*Published: Bitch Magazine Online, May 2013*

# It's Not About the Melody

I have a healthy obsession with Betty Carter; you might even call it a bit of girl crush. I am not ashamed. She has changed my whole perspective on jazz, music composition and vocal experimentation. I have never heard anyone like her. She put such a spin on jazz interpretation and syncopation and creates such unique soundscapes that I completely fall in love with her music and voice whenever I hear her.

Not everyone wants to be different. There are a number of songstresses who never wrote their own material, who never composed any music and yet rose to the heights of fame. But Carter, singing her own songs or others', just blew the top off any stage she ever stepped on.

The first songs I heard were "Once Upon A Summertime" and "Stay As Sweet As You Are" on my uncle's iPod Touch. It was loaded with Black music because he is a jazz musician. I would listen to the music while going to and from work and errands on the train in New York City. There was something about Betty Carter's voice and style and pulled me in and trapped me.

"Once Upon A Summertime" and "Stay As Sweet As You Are" make an interesting introduction to Carter's music. They're both from a late-career 1992 album called *It's Not About The Melody*, and they're soft, vulnerable and sensual. That's not exactly uncharacteristic of Carter's music, but she's better known for fast-paced, driving be-bop with complicated rhythm patterns, better exemplified by the 1990 album *Droppin' Things*.

The way she interpreted the music, the stories, the irony and humor of that album floored me. I loved the way she interpreted one of her earlier songs, "Open the Door," too, and her ability to refresh and reinvent at 60 years old was inspiring. Her music gave me something to aspire to as an artist.

Carter's live performance of "My Favorite Things" in Berlin

and her performance of "Amazon" were over-the-top and other-worldly. There are some composers and vocalist who just seem like they come from another planet or another realm. Sun Ra was that way. Nina Simone and Jimi Hendrix were that way. Betty Carter, to me, is one of the most talented and influential female jazz composers of the 20$^{th}$ century.

I am a professional singer and Carter's influence touched me. There are some artists who influenced the sounds I sing, but she influenced my musical instincts. She taught me to experiment more with my voice and to boil instrumentation down to simplistic but creative syncopation patterns.

She opened a new world to me. I hope that when I am 50 or 60 years old I will be composing complex music for handpicked band members who will create the esthetic I imagine, if not dream of. Her music has given me the confidence and vision to create a long-term musical goal for myself. I am still as obsessed with her as I was the day I first heard her music. It is a love affair that I will cherish for the rest of my life and musical career.

*Published: Hooded Utilitarian, Nov 2014*

# How Does It Feel?

**An essay about social media, introspection and telepathic connections brought on by the desperation of long distance**

In my late teens, I was thrust into obtaining a personality, and later a persona, for pure survival. After a series of rejections, and also a series of making very close friends, I was forced to make ends meet by throwing parties in arts districts. It was the only thing I could do that didn't require a degree or much experience. I just needed an attractive personality. My imagination was already so potent and fanciful from reading so many books that I could turn a room into a haven of any theme a person could muster up in their heads.

I was born to tell stories and to create worlds that would relieve people from the mundane claustrophobia of American life, but with that came great responsibility. The older I got, and the more I learned about life, the law, regulations, sex and social diplomacy, I found it important that I not get trapped in the fantasy worlds and declarations I made for my job.

Sometimes there is darkness and other times there is light. The intensity of life and my personal crusade to be authentic can bring turmoil though. Many who stand from afar appreciate my density, but up close, it can feel heavy and arduous, much like many things in life we try to keep private.

Being private in public, or being public in private, takes a healthy dose of self-awareness and will that should not be expected of others.

\* \* \*

It's getting harder and harder to hide our hearts and souls and some intellectuals speak about an awakening that is occurring in our generation. With social media, the emotional potency and public displays of private information have highlighted the pressures of social and emotional response. Love can be obtained through a screen, and telepathic connections must become realized as people struggle to maintain connections from thousands of miles away.

How does it feel? All in all, it is not much different than thousands of years that have occurred before 2014—we are all still souls living in bodies, and if you don't believe that, maybe we can agree that there is something inside of us that moves us to generally interact. We don't have to. We could do nothing, and not care, or give, or love. Nonetheless, natural selection has become a bounty of self-will, and soulmates (if you believe in them) can be overlooked because their social profile is undesirable, or they don't have the latest smart phone, the right blue jeans or an understanding of micro-societal expectations and swagger.

How do we feel? Are we making the right choices as we're driven by so many external synthetic forces? Is love pure anymore? And how sad is it that this question has to be asked? Maybe I am just guilty of exposing my own uncertainties about life, the technological revolution and all the problems I had when I was a young girl. Maybe no one else thinks about these things. I'm ok with that. No one should proclaim they have answers. When it comes to questions, though, I humbly believe we should have many.

*Published: Publik / Private, January 2014*

# Cases of Intimacy

"You got the backwash of the elixir of life."
—my homegirl, Sarah

I have been talking about a concept for an essay for a couple of days now. The short anecdote is a true and simple story, but I cannot consciously avoid beginning this piece without mentioning it, and furthermore making it the premise and foundation of a feeling I have been trying to uncover since it happened.

I woke in a puddle of someone else's drool.

In context, this not a very exciting declaration, but from my perspective, it awakened a level of perception that I thought was long-lost in my personal routine of interaction. I had forgotten what it was like to be intimate. I flew in 15 airplanes last year. I flew back and forth across the country, touring, writing and trying to find an answer to a question that may not have even been relevant at all. I have been lost for a very long time, and on the contrary have carved out a functional lifestyle and career that is purely fun and rewarding.

Drool is the root of a larger level of introspection that makes me challenge how I have been going about things. Drool is a manifestation of a matter that I never deemed to be important, and yet there it was, on my face.

I was ok about the whole thing when I thought it was my own. I had slept soundly after spending two days writing music, and socializing in a new circle that was getting familiar with me as much as I it. It was very plausible that the drool was mine, and I accepted it and wiped if off my face with the palm and back of my right hand. I was a bit astounded at the amount—I am a small person, and quietly questioned the abnormality of my sleeping pattern... I honestly cannot remember how I found out it was not my own. I cannot soundly profess that I had an intuitive realization that it trickled from someone else's head (the person who was sleeping next to me), or that I had participated in an odd conversation that drew out the answer to what seemed like an insignificant mystery moments before.

I just know something changed in me that morning, and I was fixated on the fact that in all my days, I had never let someone get close enough to me to ooze excretion on my head. That's not really my M.O.

Everyone that I mentioned this story to, even the culprit, found the situation quirky, but they understood it a lot better than I did. I felt stunted because everyone in their own way looked at me and described the scenario as "intimate," like it was a no brainer. Everyone had their own perspective, but as my friend Sarah and I talked on the telephone last night, confused and bewildered by the simplicity of our life's complications, she said, "You got the backwash of the elixir of life."

That is how we felt at the time. She had explained my simple story on such a profoundly sassy level that I had to stop and quote her.

I got the backwash of the elixir of life. Had I been cheated in some way? I know the next question that might pop into your head would be, "Well, what kind of excretion would rather have on your face?" I understand how that could be a valid question, but maybe it's just an expression of how inexperienced I really am. Inexperienced with intimacy. It doesn't matter if I am almost 30 years old, because I am here, writing and thinking about shit.

There is not really a moral to this story, or even a completely appropriate way to conclude this segment of my expression... That is why this is column. I will continue to think and write.

My last couple of essays have been about death. I am through mourning, at least for now, and I am working to explore what it is to live.

*Published: Publik / Private, June 2014*

# Angélique Kidjo:
# The Queen of Afropop Keeps Reigning

Name: Angélique Kidjo
When she started: 1981
Where she's from: Benin, Africa
Genre: World-pop, Afropop
For fans of: Akua Naru, Asa, Lila Downs
Sounds like: Afropop's global relevance

Angélique Kidjo's style of African world-pop is mesmerizingly fluid and entrancing. Considered "The Reigning Queen of Afropop" by *Afropop Worldwide* and "Africa's Premier Diva" by *Time Magazine*, her musical catalog encompasses elements of American gospel, traditional African music, and a well-honed style of world-pop that is certainly a signature of Kidjo.

In fact, the singer's music and roots span deep. Kidjo's father stems from the Fon people of Ouidah and her mother from the Yoruba people. She claims influences from American artists like Jimi Hendrix and Santana (she covers "Samba Pa Ti"), giving her touches of Latin percussion flavor that seep into the undercurrents of her work. There are countless genres and compositional elements found in Kidjo's repertoire, so that one could hear something new each time when indulging in her recordings. For example, "Eva" from her 2014 album *Eve* is one of the songs that is so sonically diverse, even nodding to the style of experimental alt-rock band Radiohead.

Listening to Angelique Kidjo's music quickly shows why she is a leading force in world-pop. This year, she snagged a Grammy Award for Best World Music Album and has won many awards for her unique takes on jazz, Latin, rumba, Afropop and American rock. She is one those phenomena that have been consistently putting out great music spanning over 30 years!

Her latest musical endeavor, *Sings,* manifests into the form of a live album where she performs with the Luxembourg Philharmonic Orchestra. Released last week (March 30), *Sings* showcases her wholesome and touching vocal chops, melding with backup singers and the full classical ensemble. She takes on a larger-than-life persona as she performs with the orchestra with confidence and ease. It's going to be very interesting to see what Angélique Kidjo does next.

*Published: MTV Iggy, April 2015*

# Saul Williams: Poetic Visionary
# Kicks Off Martyr Loser Kingdom Tour

Name: Saul Williams

When he started: 1996

Where he's from: Newburgh, New York

Genre: Alternative, experimental hip-hop

For fans of: Trent Reznor, Wax Poetic, Thavius Beck

Sounds like: Slam-poetry with drum-based, psychedelic music

Saul Williams continues to astonish fans with a month-long US tour, Martyr Loser Kingdom, which kicked off April 15. A jack of all trades, Williams has established himself in a number of facets, including musician, poet, actor and writer. He's published six books, acted in six films and released five full-length albums throughout the course of his career.

After spending the '80s to mid-'90s in Brazil studying abroad, and completing his MFA at NYU's Graduate Acting Program, Williams got his first big break in 1998 when he starred in the award-winning indie drama *Slam*. The following year, his debut book *S/HE* was published—a heartbreakingly honest and expressive account of the ending of his relationship with artist/professor Marcia Jones, who is the mother of his first child. In 2001, he released his first studio album, *Amethyst Rock Star*, setting the stage for his vibrant music career as an experimental hip-hop artist.

Williams has immersed himself in various expressive mannerisms, whether it be his fictional alter-ego, Niggy Tardust, or his newest trans-media project, Martyr Loser King. Williams told *Death and Taxes* about the makings of the latter project:

*Martyr Loser King is the name of a character like in the tradition of say... like, Niggy Tardust! I usually write, even in the books of poetry, from the perspectives of characters... I moved [to New York City] to put the play on its feet. It's a musical, and that music is the music of my next album. So it's an album, a book, and a play.*

Martyr Loser King has finally risen. He recently released two music videos and an essay in anticipation of his American tour, Martyr Loser Kingdom, featuring Sons of an Illustrious Father and Haleek Maul.

Whether he's acting in the first hip-hop Broadway play of its kind (*Holler if Ya Hear Me*, featuring the music of Tupac Shakur), writing books (*The Dead Emcee Scrolls: The Lost Teachings of Hip-Hop*), or acting in powerful indie films (*Tey (Today)*), Saul Williams is brimming with talent and incredible vision.

*Published: MTV Iggy, April 2015*

# Section Four
# Best-Of Lists and Favorite Picks

What's the best thing that happened all year? God knows why anyone asks me, but I do my best to weed out the best artists and bands that impacted the world, whether it be for one year or for fifty.

It is my honor to be such a trusted critic that my editors find it appropriate for me to name a bunch of people who did wonderfully with a long list of words. Not many freelance writers get to write "Best-Of" articles and in 2014, I wrote three. I am patted on the back.

Read these lists to see if you agree. I love music, I love sound and I love artists who go above and beyond to stand head-length above the rest in a time in our world where music is literally valued at a fraction of a dollar. I still take it seriously and personally think it's priceless.

*Arranged alphabetically by publication*

# Five Black Female Musicians
# You Should Love

Being a Black female music journalist, I have to admit that I've only written and published one article about a Black female musician in my entire career. Being an American journalist in general, it's very hard to be able to cover Black musicians that are not huge pop-stars like Rihanna and Beyoncé. I don't want to write about Rihanna and Beyoncé! I want to write about women who paved the way for today's biggest African-American female musicians.

Black female jazz and soul musicians have been composing and writing their own lyrics right along with the best musicians, to have their songs covered by white, male, British super-groups, and become overlooked and unrecognized for their genius—except through royalties. Well, I'm excited to share a little about the Black female musicians from past and present who have had a huge impact on my life, and on American and European music culture. I put together a list of five female musicians who opened the doors for Black girls like me to become whatever we want. There are women in every generation who show us how to carry ourselves, and how to find and maintain self-worth in our art, careers and lives. Black women rule! Black women are intelligent. Black women are leaders. Black women are artists, and Black women have had a hand in molding our musical culture to what it is today.

Here are five brilliant Black female musicians I love.

## Betty Carter (May 16, 1929—September 26, 1998)
I have a deep, bellowing, borderline obsession with Betty Carter. Betty was one of the best jazz improvisers and composers of the 20th century. She was a small-framed beauty whose musical legacy is larger than life. She's one of relatively few Black female

jazz composers and had a fearless knack for musical experimentation. Artists like Billie Holiday and Etta James did not write their own songs, but Ms. Betty Carter not only wrote her own lyrics, but she also hand-picked her all-male bands, trained them, taught them her music, and led them through her live performances.

She was so amazing at composing contemporary jazz music that she started a comprehensive jazz residency program for promising jazz students at the Kennedy Center in Washington DC. The program is called Betty Carter Jazz Ahead and still exists today.

### Abbey Lincoln (August 6, 1930 — August 14, 2010)

Abbey Lincoln is classy lady. She played in the 1956 film *The Girl Can't Help It* alongside Sidney Poitier, wearing a dress Marilyn Monroe wore in *Gentlemen Prefer Blondes*. She won a Golden Globe and experienced great accolades, but I know Abbey mostly from albums recorded in the last years of her life. In the 1990s, Abbey had a 10-album contract with Verve Records and fulfilled the contract in her last days. The sensual, emotional and tantalizing songs that she released from the 1990s to 2010 are said to be her best work, even though she's been recording since 1957.

Abbey's voice had a softness and sensuality that had a touch of tomboy NYC style—it's unforgettable. Her music reflected wisdom, emotional complexity and a peacefulness that cannot be duplicated. Abbey is one of a kind.

### Barbara Lynn (January 16, 1942 — )

Barbara Lynn is the quintessential feminist queen of soul. Not only did she experience success with her debut 1968 single, "You'll Lose A Good Thing," which is an amazing anthem of self-esteem, but her music has been covered by Aretha Franklin and The Rolling Stones!

In the 1960s, most female blues artists were not writing their own music. Barbara wrote most of her music and played a badass Stratocaster electric guitar in a time when the only female stars playing their own instruments were mainly country singers, who played acoustic guitars and banjos if at all. Barbara Lynn was saucy, with a natural self-confidence that never came off as cocky. She was a self-assured and beautiful musician who never complained about being different or held back.

## Skin (August 3, 1967 — )

I learned about Skin while I was in a high-school all-girls choir called The Cantadoras. I was singing next to a bleach-blonde skater girl who looked over at me and said, "You sing like Skunk Anansie!" Being a 16-year-old Black American girl, I had no idea who the female-fronted British metal band Skunk Anansie was. The second I got home from school, I jumped on Napster and listened to Skunk Anansie's songs, falling in love with the voice of lead singer Skin. Her voice is gorgeous, full, powerful, and painfully authentic. First, it was an honor to be compared to her, but it was her beauty and style that truly struck me.

Skin is also a brave and candid musical artist who has opened up about her journey of coming out as bisexual woman. She is an amazing role model for strength and gives a touching and realistic tone to the realities of bisexuality.

## Kandi Burruss (May 17, 1976 — )

I know I'm going to get hell for this one — lots of people probably only know Kandi from her part on the reality TV series *Real Housewife of Atlanta*. But don't judge too harshly! She's single, raising a child on her own, and is an independently wealthy music-industry powerhouse. Kandi was the first African-American woman to win ASCAP's songwriter of the year. She wrote TLC's urban-feminist hit, "No Scrubs," and the other famous urban-feminist hit song, Destiny Child's "Bills Bills Bills."

She's also worked with top country artist Martina McBride, showing her ability to write for and with women from different creeds and musical genres.

Kandi has been an amazing influence on me. While she's on a show that praises gold diggers, she's always maintained her independence in her music and in her personal life.

*Published: Bitch Magazine Online, April 2013*

# Five Albums You Should Be Listening To Right Now: The Process Records

### 1. Bad Liquor Pond, *Blue Smoke Orange Sky* (2012)

Bad Liquor Pond's mellow-dramatic take on '60s psychedelic rock is sexy and hypnotizing. Although this Baltimore-based band is mainly worshiped by a small (but loyal) pool of neo-psych-rock enthusiasts, *Blue Smoke Orange Sky*'s down-to-earth shoegazey temperament should appeal to anyone with the proverbial pulse. Never underestimate the power of psychedelia—this music bypasses the head and drives straight for the soul.

### 2. Romantic States, *A Shell Is Born* (2011)

*A Shell Is Born* is an endearing, introspective album. Sonically skeletal but still lush with the possibilities of love, this is a triumphant effort from two electronically-inclined singer/songwriters whose take on love in the new millennium is coyly atmospheric, but focused. *A Shell Is Born* also showcases an amazing cover of Johnny Cash's "Ring of Fire."

### 3. Betty Carter, *Droppin' Things* (1990)

Betty Carter is an old-school, sadly recondite jazz composer and vocalist. Her adventurous 1990 release *Droppin' Things* exhibits her wide-ranging musical expression, and deep understanding of improvisation. Betty's style sets her apart from many of the safe, clean-cut songstresses of her era—this somber and nostalgic album could be described as Billie Holiday-esque... if Holiday was completely, eccentrically off-kilter. Carter even reinterprets her own early masterpiece, "Open The Door," thirty years later on *Droppin' Things*, turning the song into a post-modern jazz classic.

## 4. A Tribe Called Quest, *The Love Movement* (1998)

*The Love Movement* is one of the most underappreciated albums in hip-hop history. This epic, 21-track set of tried-and-true hip-hop songs displays Tribe's maturity with polished beats and rhymes from Phife and Q-Tip, as well as a few brash collaborations with Busta Rhymes during a very... "overt" stage in his career. *The Love Movement* was the perfect end to A Tribe Called Quest's artistic journey, and should be appreciated as a classy and well-meaning record.

## 5. The Brian Jonestown Massacre, *Their Satanic Majesties' Second Request* (1996)

*Their Satanic Majesties' Second Request* came to us after gestating in a human-like being who was sent to this planet to teach our children how to write brilliant rock and roll. This humanoid is called Anton Newcombe, and, along with his bright but troubled bandmates, he released a plethora of albums that effortlessly outdid their musical peers for most of the late '90s. This is a massive, 19-track record that bends the rules of modern rock and roll. Shut up, listen, and completely give yourself over to *Second Request* and the world it sucks you into.

*Published: Nerve.com, February 2013*

*Jordannah's firm, The Process Records and TPR-Mag.com, was a leader in independent blogging and music criticism in 2010–2012*

# The 15 Albums of 2014 You Should Be Listening to Right Now: New Releases

2014 has been a great year for music—even the experimental-pop debuts, along with some ancient comebacks. Because we admire pop power just as much as indie cred, here are 15 of the best mainstream new releases of the year. Keep your fingers crossed that the new year delivers bigger, better, louder, sexier and more unique tracks.

## 1. Julian Casablancas + The Voidz, *Tyranny*

Casablancas has been working over the last number of years to find his own musical voice after releasing a solo album in 2009. Nonetheless, Julian Casablancas has emerged with a new band called The Voidz. *Tyranny* is an odd and heavy rock album flaunting boisterous ebbs and flows, but keeping Casablancas' signature walking-bassline sound which is especially prevalent in the track "Human Sadness." *Tyranny* gives you a chance to hear Casablancas sing with conviction, performing more complicated vocal rhythms, and his range is insane. *Tyranny* is a triumphant and exhilarating album.

## 2. Leonard Cohen, *Popular Problems*

Cohen's sultry, soulful new album is as smooth as cream on a summer's day. *Popular Problems* takes you on an intentionally smooth, gradual ride telling stories of pain, suffering and hope. Cohen's gravelly voice is controlled and completely mesmerizing. He draws you in with his wisdom and the soulful contemporary instrumentals keeps you wanting more.

## 3. Common, *Nobody's Smiling*

The Chicago-based hip-hop royal has released a brilliant and confident album. *Nobody's Smiling* is an instant classic taking you back to the '90s golden era of rap music. Common keeps getting better and better over the years. *Nobody's Smiling* is a satisfying hip-hop effort.

## 4. King Woman, *Dove / Fond Affections*

Kristina Esfandiari of Miserable snuck in a new release from her solo project, King Woman. *Dove / Fond Affections* is a follow-up to Esfandiari's *Degrida / Sick Bed* single—this 2014 release is sensual and soothingly creative. "Fond Affections" is a cover of the Rema Rema song and is an ambient and femininely washed-out version of the 1980 track. King Woman certainly puts her own touch on the experimental pop song. "Dove" is a wild and noisy art song that displays King Woman's genius. There's not much more to say after the word genius emerges.

## 5. Beck, *Morning Phase*

After a slew of lukewarm albums, *Morning Phase* was a surprise to Beck fans and the press at large when he went back to the roots of his singer/songwriter talents and wrote the most honest, tastefully ethereal electro-acoustic album in a decade. *Morning Phase* is a flawless effort that never goes too far right or left when it comes to Beck's Neil Young-esque psych-folk songs, keeping the entire album grounded and listenable. You never want to skip a track, you never want to miss a thing on *Morning Phase*. The album draws you in and keeps you digging for jewel after jewel from beginning to end.

## 6. Swans, *To Be Kind*

This 121-minute indie-rock opus is intriguing particularly because every song on the record is over 5 minutes long. You've got to be invested in this album and give into this music art installation to make it through. The album is gorgeous and a work of pure creativity, producing tracks that make you feel like you're sitting in a live studio session with Swans as they build upon repetitious riffs tearing themselves away from 20 years of previous works and going on a search for true rock enlightenment.

## 7. Xiu Xiu, *Angels Guts: Red Classroom*

*Angel Guts: Red Classroom* is a brilliantly strange album, creating minimalist John Cage-style sound expressions in its opening track, "Angel Guts," and dragging you down a rabbit hole of eerie art-rock. If Xiu Xiu doesn't give you goose bumps and an air of paranoia, you're not listening to this album loudly enough. *Angel Guts* gives you what you expect from this slightly horrifying and arousing band.

## 8. Prince, *Art Official Age*

Prince has returned with a funky and danceable R&B-pop album. Prince's 13th studio album is youthful, sexy and encompasses his humorous and fun-loving spirit. It's hard not to fall in love with this album because this Prince stays true to himself musically. The album is real, enjoyable and completely unpretentious.

## 9. Frank Ocean, *Memrise* (single)

We've waited and waited. Frank Ocean is one of the most refreshing and exciting musicians on the planet and in R&B history. I know that sounds dramatic, but it's true. Ocean dropped a tiny little stroke of perfection called "Memrise" in the last month of 2014. The lo-fi one-minute track left a salivating emblem of hope and a promise of more art for the future. "Memrise" is not an album… it may not even be a full song, but it is more than worth mentioning.

## 10. Shabazz Palaces, *Lese Majesty*

Shabazz Palaces' *Lese Majesty* has birthed the dawn of a new genre-obliterating era which may not fully emerge as a full-on musical revolution for a number of years. Nonetheless, *Lese Majesty* is a direct assault on the current hip-hop status quo, creating psychedelic-electronic instrumental beats, mixed with live percussion and instrumental ornamentation. This Seattle-based duo flaunt their skills creating painstakingly elaborate and layered songs that are still danceable and rhythmically practical.

## 11. The Brian Jonestown Massacre, +-

Anton Newcombe's 2013 full album, *Revelation,* could have easily made it to the list, but the shotgun release of the follow up EP, +-, slipped in at the end of the year and proved to be a pleasant surprise. The Brian Jonestown Massacre's coherent current sound is coming from a solid mold. +- is majorly touching and relatable. It's always great to watch BJM go through different stages of sound and experimentation. This album is full of strong, contemplated and satisfying tracks.

## 12. St. Vincent, *St. Vincent*

The highly anticipated 2014 release of St. Vincent's self-titled album did not disappoint. With collaborations with artists like Sharon Jones & The Dap-Kings' drummer Homer Steinweiss, the album is impressively eccentric. *St. Vincent* borders on noise-pop and math-rock, showcasing strange and fast-paced arrangements that morph and change throughout each track.

## 13. D'Angelo and The Vanguard, *Black Messiah*

2014's Christmas miracle came in the form of the return of the illuminating soul musician, D'Angelo. Always regarded as a true musical gift from the clouds, D'Angelo emerged almost out of nowhere with a full-length album entitled *Black Messiah*. This new album is much more political than D'Angelo's earlier work, but his transcendent R&B-soul style remains only to become more refined, making D'Angelo's genius concretely understood as more than just a two-album fluke. *Black Messiah* is moving and spiritual and goes above and beyond the call of duty of pop music.

## 14. Ariel Pink, *Pom Pom*

Ariel Pink's *Pom Pom* is a refreshing indie-pop album that is fun and sticks out like a beautiful swollen sore thumb against Pink's alternative-mainstream counterparts. *Pom Pom* plays with well-produced lo-fi echoes, '60s-style and post-modern instrumental mashups and a great sense of humor. This is one of those albums for the underground music lovers who grew up with the artists they were drawn to when they bought their first indie albums.

## 15. FKA Twigs, *LP1*

In the tradition of the new experimental-pop movement (Grimes, Shabazz Palaces, Lorde, St. Vincent), FKA Twigs' *LP1* took the American music world by storm. The British art-pop musician created an echoing, off-syncopated R&B record that is equally as sexy as it is unique. Her beautiful voice drapes perfectly over her, at times, awkwardly composed pop songs. *LP1* is a respectable and refreshing effort.

*Published: Nerve.com, December 2014*

*The order of the list does not reflect Jordannah's preference or favor of each album. No shade to Nerve.com. We love you long time!*

# Top 10 Hip-Hop Albums of 2014

Even though we live in a time of radio-ready music that's shallower than a starfish wading pool, there are some hip-hop artists who make an effort to show individual style and attempt to express real glimpses of worldly perspective. If 2014 can be considered a year that sits in the midst of the "dark era of hip-hop," here are a few shining beacons of light that are, though mainstream, either making boisterously prevalent and competent returns, consistent solid releases or harrowing debuts.

### 10. Wiz Khalifa, *Blacc Hollywood*

Wiz Khalifa's *Blacc Hollywood* exhibits a combination of glamor and south-coast hip-hop swagger that makes this record interesting. Khalifa will sing on a pop track like "Promises," then share a track with Southern hip-hop aficionados Juicy J and Project Pat of Three 6 Mafia on "KK." *Blacc Hollywood* is the fifth studio album from the young rapper, but there is still a major presence of youthfulness to the album that doesn't come off as pretentious or irritating. The record just stays fresh and green as if it were sealed in a Ziploc bag.

### 9. Pharrell Williams, *Girl*

Whether you like Pharrell as a solo artist or not, he takes you into an odd dream-world of pop music that he created all on his own. *Girl* is a simplistically jubilant album that includes his monster hit, "Happy." Williams is always going to be relevant, and *Girl* brings a lighthearted collection of songs to a genre that is usually filled with cocky anthems and dark imagery.

### 8. Nas, *Illmatic XX*

Twenty years after the illuminating, classic hip-hop album *Illmatic* was released, Sony Legacy assembled a duel-disc special-edition release of the album, entitled *Illmatic XX*. Though this compilation did not receive great reviews, it exists for an honorable purpose: to respect and commemorate an album that ushered one of the realest and wisest MCs into households across the world.

## 7. Pharoahe Monch, *PTSD*

Pharoahe Monch's *PTSD* is a strange themed album that touches on the subjects of mental illness, addiction and redemption. Monch does a great job painting a picture of what it's like to be unstable and having the desire to crawl out of the depths of despair. The album is disturbing, thought-provoking and well produced. *PTSD* never loses sight of the story it sets out to tell, making it a coherent work of art.

## 6. Mobb Deep, *The Infamous Mobb Deep*

So good. After eight years of silence from the gritty, Queens-based hip-hop duo, Mobb Deep re-emerges with a triumphant return and an ill album. *The Infamous Mobb Deep* is a deluxe album that gifts listeners with 17 tracks of original music plus a second disc of unreleased material from the recording sessions of their highly acclaimed second album, *The Infamous*. Mobb Deep are known for their violent and intelligent requiems of street life. This album holds nothing back and is crisp and flawless.

## 5. Common, *Nobody's Smiling*

Common is a constant that keeps you coming back for more. The Chicago-based hip-hop staple creates a passionate and vivid album with *Nobody's Smiling*. Listening to Common makes you wonder how today's hip-hop listeners can be so frivolous and listen to any new artist that comes out the gate. Common raps with discernment and brings a level of class and refinement to the game. *Nobody's Smiling* contains cameos from Lil' Herb, Big Sean and Malik Yusef, bringing even more taste and unneeded but respectable credibility to it.

## 4. The Roots, *And Then You Shoot Your Cousin*

The Roots is another example of an artist who always delivers. *And Then You Shoot Your Cousin* brings surprisingly strong tracks like "Never" and the Elton John/Otis Redding-esque track "Tomorrow." The album adopts a number of R&B latent tracks, grabbing music from the past then rushing forward as they touch on more modern and experimental pop elements. The album is as touching and authentic as you would expect.

## 3. Lil' Kim, *Hardcore 2K14*

Lil' Kim's five-track mixtape, *Hardcore 2K14*, was surrounded by speculation and delays. Nonetheless, it always was and always will be obvious that Kim is fabulous. *Hardcore 2K14* does nothing but highlight Kim's staggering flow and great choices in collaborators. Her solo track, "Identity Theft," is as solid as a rock. It's so interesting that it took her so long to drop new music because she's so powerful as a lyricist that her music seems effortless. She raps on *2K14* like she does it every day and in her sleep.

## 2. Azealia Banks, *Broke With Expensive Taste*

Azealia Banks finally put her money where her mouth was this year with an impressive debut release. Banks has serious style, and by not slouching or rushing on *Broke With Expensive Taste*, she showed the world that she has the ability to produce great records. The album is ambitious. She's a young artist, but the album is mature and full of depth while dripping with professionalism. Tracks such as "Desperado" are dark and sensuous. Her deep and well-trained vocal persona is a force to be reckoned with.

## 1. Shabazz Palaces, *Lese Majesty*

Shabazz Palaces' album *Lese Majesty* is a resuscitation of modern hip-hop. It's a bucket of cold water to the face, forcing hip-hop listeners and MCs to wake up and look at music and the world from an entirely different perspective. This record is a psychedelic opus that swirls elements of jazz, live African/international percussion beats and ill rhymes into one groundbreaking album. The otherworldly hip-hop duo made it no secret that their attempts to stand out from the rest are not only intentional but also a challenge to the current leaders of the genre to take note and fear the transcendent and intensely original pastiche of sounds *Lese Majesty* is bringing to the table.

*Published: New York Amsterdam News, December 2014*

# Section Five
# Interviews

Conversation. They say that some people learn by hearing and other people learn by seeing. Some people need repetition to learn things. It's also been said that women process their feelings and information by speaking and men are more internal about processing things.

I love to talk to people. I am curious and full of questions and I like to ask off-the-cuff questions because I know all the rock and rap stars I talk to can give up to 20 interviews in a day. In order to write a great piece, I've got to be random while staying slightly on topic.

I don't know. I try not to think too much. There are times when I don't research the artist at all so I can dig for pearls of an artist's process and consciousness with a clean slate. Information is not everything. It becomes particularly less valuable when it comes from anywhere else but the horse's mouth. The best source you have is the artist.

*Arranged alphabetically by interviewee*

# Ishmael Butler

## Won't Black Down: Ishmael Butler of Shabazz Palaces Takes a Royal Stance in His Music

Whether he's in the pop spotlight or on hip-hop's experimental fringe, Ishmael Butler of Shabazz Palaces accepts his position with humility. Soon after winning a Grammy in 1993 as part of the popular jazz/hip-hip outfit Digable Planets, the group broke up and Butler, then known as Butterfly, fell into near obscurity.

More than a decade and a half later, Butler re-emerged with a renewed sense of creativity, releasing two critically acclaimed EPs as Shabazz Palaces followed by the full-length *Black Up* on the legendary punk label Sub Pop Records. In Shabazz Palaces, Butler dropped his previous group's jazz vocabulary for wildly experimental excursions into hip-hop, rock and psychedelia. Last year, Shabazz Palaces returned with *Lese Majesty*, which continues the sonic and poetic experimentation Butler's long been known for.

In conversation, Butler is soft-spoken, often giving simple, one-word replies and long pauses that say as much about his thought process as do his words. Fortunately, when we talked to Butler in anticipation of Shabazz Palaces' April 5 show at The Chapel, he was open about everything from his thoughts on royalty and politics to working with Jack White, Flying Lotus and Herbie Hancock (though not all at the same time).

\* \* \*

**Speaking of *Lese Majesty*, there was a highly publicized case of lese majesty [the crime of insulting a monarch] in Thailand in February, after a Thai college student put on a satirical play called *The Wolf Bride* and was sentenced to two and a half years in jail. Did you know lese majesty was still an active law?**

Yeah, but I mean, it's not literal. Lese Majesty, the Shabazz Palaces album, is artwork, it's not political. Using the term as the literal interpretation and application, nah, it's not that. We're talking about a different royalty and a different concept and perception of it that has more to do with the entertainment "state" that we live in more than what they're dealing with in Thailand. I hope people don't take it literally, like we're trying to offend the majesty of the ruling class in Thailand.

I was just being a nerd. I'm not sure if the controversy over that particular lese majesty sentence is common knowledge here in America.

That same fascism is here. It exists here, whether it is in music or the government or the police force.

**Since the release of your new album, it seem you've participated in some interesting shows and collaborations, one of which was Shabazz Palaces playing at Jack White's Third Man Records in January. What was it like to work with him?**

He really has a family setup there with him and his staff. They all obviously get along and know each other. As a social environment, [Third Man Records] is special because of the family atmosphere and the deservedly legendary mystique and aura that is around Jack himself. The facilities are very unique. That night, we played and recorded and it goes to tape right there. It's a very unique and rare musical experience. It was pretty much the most unique thing I've been involved with. It was really cool. You go and perform and they release the live performance on Third Man Records.

**You shared a photo on Instagram of you, Herbie Hancock and Flying Lotus. What was going on that night?**

Well, I was in Los Angeles and I was at Flying Lotus' house working on some music. He called Herbie. He and Herbie have been tight after getting to know each other the last couple of years since Herbie [played on the Flying Lotus album] *You're Dead*. He came over and we were just there, making music. Then later that night, we went to get some food. That's how it went down.

**Why haven't you talked publicly about your collaborations and working with Flying Lotus? Is it early in the development stage of you making music with him?**

Nah, it's just out of respect. People might not want to talk about it. If you're working on music, it only matters if it comes out and people get to hear it. Until then, to me, there's nothing to talk about, so you go around and work with people and get ideas and develop relationships and friendships. But in terms of sitting around and saying, "I'm doing this and I'm doing that," it's ridiculous to me. If we finish stuff and it comes out, that would be the only time I would feel comfortable talking about it because there are other people involved.

**You're playing five dates with Flying Lotus on your upcoming European tour. Do those dates have anything to do with you currently working with Flying Lotus in the studio?**

No, it doesn't have anything to do with us working with Flying Lotus. He's doing a tour over there and we have always talked about doing some shows together, so it's through his initiative and power to invite us to do some shows with him, but we were already going to tour at this time. To be able to be added to a few of his bills is cool.

**You've surrounded yourself with a lot of super-talented people—like Khalil Joseph, the visual artist who created the amazing music video for your "Belhaven Meridian." Do you feel like a sort of magnet for creativity?**

I've been fortunate to work with creative, exciting people with a lot of imagination and integrity that really have a lot essential emotions for their artistic endeavors. It's good that they are getting recognized for it, but I know all those people were putting the same amount of energy and passion into what they were doing before they got the recognition. The real special thing about them is the fact that they just live and breathe the things that they make.

**If money wasn't an issue, what would be your dream project?**
[Thoughtfully repeats the question to himself.] Probably to have a really cool recording studio on a beach in a place where it is sunny and there are cloudless skies and water. I would invite people to come and spend time and record there for whatever amount of time they could spare and stay. That sounds fantastic to me.

*Published: SF Weekly, April 2015*

# Jason Simon

## Jason Simon on His Musical Balancing Act

Jason Simon, of the illustrious stoner-rock band Dead Meadow, has been experimenting with his solo work and different sound-scapes since the release of his self-titled debut in 2010. While embarking on the journey of showcasing his stripped-down folk ballads, Simon found himself innocently inviting his friends to play as back-up for his live performances. Those live perfor-mances prompted him to create a full and semi-permanent band of musicians consisting of Oakley Munson, Ryan Raspys, Jessica Senteno and Nate Ryan (formerly of The Black Angels), and he named this collaborative affair Old Testament.

I got to see Old Testament live in Los Angeles earlier this year, and all I can express is that Jason is a solid, quiet and confident songwriter. The elements of Appalachian folk music and post-modern neo-psych rock make the band tonally unique. There's something to be said about Simon breaking from the 15-year consistency of putting his main efforts into Dead Meadow, and now going out and creating music that no one is doing in L.A. with Old Testament.

Simon has been one of my favorite people to talk to over the past couple years, particularly because of his personal creative renaissance that could be considered a journey of musical self-expression and experimentation more than anything. He took the time to talk to me about the balance he experiences between completing his new Dead Meadow effort, and taking the time to manifest Old Testament into a live and recording musical project.

\* \* \*

## What sparked the formation of Old Testament?

It came from the solo performances I was doing as Jason Simon and the release of that record. I would grab musicians from in and around Los Angeles, to play with me on stage. I started playing with Oakley Munson who plays harmonica and bass, and Ryan Raspys, and he would come and play drums. They are both such cool, rad musicians that I thought we should just become a band.

I wanted to do something more than just perform under the name "Jason Simon." I think it's cooler to perform under a name other than my own. So, Old Testament just grew from there. Jessica has been playing harmonium with us, and now Nate Ryan, who used to be in The Black Angels, comes and plays with us from time to time, when he's around.

**So you're never going to do a solo record again?**

I don't know, I probably will. I'm just taking it one day at a time. It's cool because we're finishing the Old Testament record and the Dead Meadow record is all done, we're just completing the mixing. So now I can concentrate on completing the Old Testament album. The basic tracks for the Old Testament record were recorded last November, so now we're going to finish everything up.

**Why did you name your new band Old Testament?**

I guess the vibe we were trying to invoke was from Oakley and I listening to a lot of old Americana and old-time Appalachian banjo music. We were into that slightly creepy style that you get from musicians like Dock Boggs, and their songs with these tales, these stories that are bizarre, far-out and weird. The songs kind of had this Old Testament flavor. You know, tales of vengeance and retribution, love and lust, so we were thinking we would go for a band name that had a slight Old Testament feel, and after a while, we were just like, we should go bold with it, and just call the band Old Testament. I'm a fan of the weird tale, and there's nothing weirder than the stories of the Old Testament.

**It's true. Epic stories like *Harry Potter*, *Lord of the Rings* and Shakespeare's tragedies have a hard time holding a candle to the drama, murder and incest of the stories of the Old Testament...**

Definitely, and tracing the history to the old American ballads I've been listening to, they turn out to be old Scottish ballads and crop up from stories that have been told in different times and places, which were passed from one generation to the next. They are songs that surround the central issues of life here on this planet.

**And Townes Van Zandt has been an influence on your music as well?**

I went through a big Townes phase a couple of years back. He's just a great songwriter.

**It's understood that Old Testament was influenced by folk, bluegrass and Appalachian music, but it's also obvious that your music is doused with touches of post-modern compositional styles and psychedelia.**

Especially when we started playing with a band of five people, we didn't come off like we were trying to play folk. For me, in regards to Dead Meadow, it's like we plan to work on a very simple song, and with Dead Meadow being a three-piece band, it's likely to have to add a lot to the music to make a full soundscape. With five people in Old Testament, I can just lay back in the cut, and play some chords and just carry a tune, you know? I feel like most of the members of Old Testament are intuitive players. The sound does kind of fall into place.

**What are your criteria when choosing bandmates? Do you choose them intuitively?**

When I was playing solo shows, I would invite friends to play shows with me, and then they'd play and I'd think "Yeah, that was really cool." So, yeah I think it is an intuitive thing. It's good to have people adding their own parts because it's more alive that way, as opposed to working out parts for other people, but at the same time, you want everything to conform to a certain vision.

**In regards to Old Testament being based on folk and Americana, and Dead Meadow being rooted in stoner rock and roll, which style comes easier to you, folk or psychedelia?**

I just kind of write songs, and I'll be playing and think, "Oh, this could go with Dead Meadow or this would work for Old Testament." They kind of end up converging a lot, the songs are not that different. What I like about the old-time folk stuff is that the music is still really trippy and far out. So, in a way, they are branches from the same tree.

**...and that "tree" is you, as the core songwriter?**

Yeah, I guess so.

**I didn't know that you wrote the songs for Dead Meadow, I thought the music was more of a collaborative situation.**

These days, the songs come from me, but the songs get changed a lot and just from us all coming together and playing. It becomes a Dead Meadow song from all of us jamming on it.

**Personally, I've never really seen other musicians play the guitar the way you do, and as well as you do, and I wonder if it bothers you that you don't receive as much recognition for your stellar technical guitar playing.**

I think it all comes in time. That can't be something to be concerned with. Either way, if you're looking for it, or concerned you don't have it, it's not going to be something that's going to lead to happiness. And guitarists that I like, of course I like Jimi Hendrix and Jimmy Page, but people like Stacey Sutherland of 13 Floor Elevators, of course he gets recognition, but the guy plays some of the coolest stuff ever. I like guitarists that are off the beaten track, things that are a little weirder. I'm happier being a part of that niche.

**Is it too early to ask when the first Old Testament album will be completed?**

We're going to try to finish it in the next couple of weeks, and the Dead Meadow record will be out in September. The reissue of the first Dead Meadow record should be out in July. I think Matador is planning on putting out reissues of Dead Meadow as well, and we'll probably release Old Testament through Xemu Records.

*Published: The Wild Magazine, June 2013*

# Jodie Smith

## Jodie Smith's Educated Approach

U.K.-born top model Jodie Smith initially intrigued me because she seemed to be recognized throughout the industry by top fashion media outlets and blogs in a way I'd never seen before.

Even the most popular, young, social-media-savvy models with jobs lined up every week don't appear to receive the same type of attention for their intellect and back story.

I caught up with Jodie, because I wanted to know how she rose to such a prominent position in the industry and molded her persona to peak the curiosity of journalists and top agencies alike. My conversation was enlightening, a discussion filled with thought-provoking advice. She's definitely one-of-a-kind.

\* \* \*

**Most models in the industry don't get a lot of interviews from the press. What do you think it is about you that attracts the media on an intellectual level?**

Before I started in the creative industry, I came [out] of an educational background. As a "know-it-all," I always have a lot to say. I think what sets me apart is that when people do ask me what I think about something, they hear something intelligent come out. I think that's what gets people to want to know about what I have to say about things.

**Do you believe the stereotype about models being less intelligent is true?**

I wouldn't say as a whole that models are less intelligent. A lot of the models are really young, or discovered from a small town, and don't always continue their education, and grow to live this charmed life. They get to travel and experience a lot of things, but they also are in an industry where they don't get asked many questions about what they think as a model. They kind of want you to be a blank canvas.

If you start when you're 15 or 16 years old, you start working a job before you're really a woman, and are discovering who you are while being shown as someone who is more grown-up than you actually are.

**What is your educational background?**
I have a degree in finance.

**Who are your favorite designers?**
I'm a big fan of Christopher Bailey, and Burberry, being a British brand—I love everything that it represents.

**Another interesting thing about the interviews you've done is that the publications rarely highlight your race, whereas models of color are usually tagged by their ethnicities. Models like Tyra Banks and Iman have found this stigma to be a concern. Why do you think your race is overlooked in your features?**
Well, I think that whether or not anyone is writing about it, it's always something that's going to come up. When any model goes to a casting meeting, the model they send is based on requirements from that agency. The designer may have an idea about what they want the girl to look like, so I don't think that's going to change any time soon.

In terms of why things are different now, compared to when Tyra Banks and Iman were modeling, it's what we're in, an age of personal branding and social media, which really allows an individual to control how they're talked about and perceived by other people. People can go along on your journey with you and follow along with whatever your definition of yourself is.

**How do you carry yourself when you arrive to go-sees (castings)?**
Not only am I a Black woman, but I also have a dark complexion. I always joke and say that my skin tone walks into the room before I do. It announces itself before I say anything. So, when I

walk in a room, I have to be Jodie Smith.

**Is modeling your passion?**

I feel like I'm in a coming-of-age phase right now. I love it. I enjoy what I do and am blessed to be able to do what I do.

**Since you have a degree in finance, do you plan on going back into that field later on in your life, or do you plan on staying in the fashion industry?**

I had to be a corporate banker for 8 months to realize that's not what I wanted to do. My goal is to have a career that stretches over decades. I don't think there is a girl who doesn't want that, but while I am modeling, I am pursuing other things. I am beginning to get into writing and acting. I am learning what I am into right now.

**Do you have any advice for young models?**

It's important for any model that is going to start modeling to figure out who you are before you get started. People are going to ask you for an emotion that you cannot always yet possibly understand. If you're playing this kind of game of pretending, and the process is beyond your experience, it's very easy to get lost.

**What is your WILD wish?**

I'd like to have a busy show season starting in February, a television role and my first major feature-film role!

*Published: The Wild Magazine, October 2013*

# Jo Mersa

## The Next Rising Marley Star

*I had to show to my father that I wanted it. It's not because I am a Marley and it's a part of the "family business," it's not about that. I have to make sure that it comes from the heart.*

Jo Mersa Marley was born into a family like no other. As the eldest son of Stephen Marley and the grandson of the legendary reggae star, Bob Marley, Jo Mersa continues his family's musical legacy with humor and humility.

At 24 years old, he's currently on tour promoting the compilation *Set Up Shop, Vol. 2*, which features several of his Marley relatives and label-mates at Ghetto Youth International. Released last December, the compilation has already proven to be a hit, peaking at number 1 on the US Billboard Reggae Album chart. His contribution is "Rock and Flow," which also doubles on the rising Jamaican star's debut EP, *Comfortable*. The track permeates positivity, while making one's body sway to the feel-good, vintage-reggae vibes.

We spoke to Jo Mersa over the phone in between gigs about what it's like touring without his father for the first time, how positivity transcends, and fighting for what deserves to be fought for.

\* \* \*

**You're on tour supporting the compilation you feature in, *Set Up Shop, Vol. 2*. What is the main message that this album and Ghetto Youth International are working to share with the world?**
The message is love. It's about love with your friends or your

family. It's about society learning to love one another more. There are many different ways of explaining it, but it's about making sure you love what you do and work hard. It's all about love and loving in many different ways.

**How is it being on tour right now? Are you very close with all the guys on the compilation?**

Yeah. We're family and label-mates. We're like brothers.

**When are you planning to drop a solo record?**

Well, we released a song on the compilation, which is also on my EP that is entitled *Comfortable*. The single is called, "Rock and Swing." I'm currently working on my next album, a full LP. But right now, we're deciding which song we're going to push out next. We'll probably push out one or two more songs and music videos from the EP, and then we'll start to release songs from the LP that I've been working on. I've been performing some of the music I've been working on live. I've been giving sneak previews [of my upcoming music] on this tour.

**Is this your first tour? Have you been on the road before?**

Yeah, I've been on tour many times with my father. This is my first tour by myself [performing] with the Ghetto Youth Crew.

**You're on tour without supervision!**

Supervision, no. It's not supervision, he's still my father, and I'm a grown man [laughs]. I will say it is a different experience [being on tour without my father], but it is an experience I have to have. It's a wonderful thing and never a dull moment with this crew.

**After spending much of your life on tour and in the studio, do you feel the life you live and the music you make is natural for you, or did you have to work at it?**

You have to believe in something and have a lot of ambition and drive in you and love it. I must say that I've done my fair share of hard work. It wasn't easy for me. My father told me, just because I wanted to do music, it didn't mean that everything was going to drop in my lap. I couldn't go into the studio until I started understanding what Pro Tools is and what an interface is.

I had to know how the speakers and how the mixing board worked. I had to know a little about guitar, drums and how to play the bass. Drums are my favorite thing. But I had to work [at music]. I had to show to my father that I wanted it. It's not because I am a Marley and it's a part of the "family business," it's not about that. I have to make sure that it comes from the heart.

**If you had to make a choice and take any job other than music, what would it be?**

I think it would be two things: I enjoy making people laugh and I enjoy cooking. There were times when I was really thinking about going to school for cooking, and run a restaurant, the whole works.

**What do you have coming up this year?**

We have another tour coming up in August. We have a lot coming up. I have some more collaborations coming with my father. We have a lot going on right now.

**How do you find peace when you're so busy? Do you require privacy?**

I require privacy. Who doesn't? At the same time, I believe peace comes from within one's self. Peace flows. My good vibe travels and makes others' vibes better. Positivity comes across and transcends. You have to make sure your thinking isn't negative.

**Well, thanks for speaking to us, Jo Mersa!**

Oh, wait. I have one more thought about one of your questions. There are actually three things I would do with my life: I would do comedy, I would open up a restaurant, and I would be a lawyer. I would fight for what deserves to be fought for. I have been inspired by many great lawyers. There are many things that I would fight for that I won't get into at the moment, but yes, that would be another thing I would do.

*Published: MTV Iggy, April 2015*

# Peter Daltrey

## An In-Depth Interview with Peter Daltrey

Peter Daltrey is a titan among men in regards to the incredible scope of his musical influence since the 1960's with his bands Kaleidoscope and Fairfield Parlour. This spring, Daltrey is embarking on an American tour as a Kaleidoscope featuring: Rob Bartholomew Campanella (The Brian Jonestown Massacre, Quarter After) on Bass; Cheryl Caddick (Silver Phial) on drums; Nick Castro (Young Elders, Poison Tree) on mellotron and rhythm guitar; Christof Certik (Young Elders, Winter Flowers) on lead guitar, to promote and share his incredible presence within a rock culture that he helped create.

This legend was kind enough to relay his incredible history and thoughts. It's a complete honor to have the opportunity to share his story with you.

\* \* \*

**Let's talk about *Tangerine Dream* by Kaleidoscope. Quoted letter from John Abbey: "Kaleidoscope are sweeter than Pink Floyd, not so bitter as The Beatles and have more talent." This album is like a well-kept secret in the psych scene. How do you perceive it? What were you trying to do and did it come across?** First off, I'm not sure about that quote. The Beatles were bitter…? The Beatles were our role models. In the sixties everything revolved around the Beatles. We all looked to them for changes in fashion, hairstyles and music. Their songwriting heavily influenced us. Everyone was trying to keep up with their startling progress.

Ed and I just wrote the best songs we could. We had been writing ever since the band started in 1964. But l think it was in

'66 that we began writing real original material. Before that most had simply been a pastiche of blues and pop all rolled into one. But after we heard Revolver, and much of the early Bee Gees material, our own writing style evolved into what is called psychedelia.

We never intentionally set out to be psychedelic; we were simply reflecting the mood of the time in my lyrics and Ed's music. Fontana signed us on the strength of our songwriting, but the song that actually secured us a one-year recording contract was the poppy "Holiday Maker." But once our producer, Dick Leahy, heard us play him "Flight from Ashiya" one day in his office he insisted Fontana sign us to a five-year contract.

Dick was very excited about the album and encouraged us to be inventive. We responded in the only way we knew how, by improving our song-writing. We were actually recording the album during the summer of '67, the very height of the short-lived period of psychedelia. What were we trying to achieve…? We were attempting to make the very best record that we could. It was as simple as that.

Because of poor distribution our first single, printed in a full-color photo sleeve—remarkable for a first single from a new band—failed to sell which resulted in a loss of publicity for our first album. And so it slipped away quietly. Lying dormant in a dusty corner of history until the eighties and nineties when new generations dug it up and loved what they heard.

Justification for all the toil and tears we spent in making it twenty years before.

**What is the story of your artistic vision and your interaction with your record label? At one point you were touring with The Who, Arthur Brown and Fairport Convention, then you go back to the studio and you're broke? The Noel-Gay agency failed to provide you with enough live work to keep you financially looked after? How did you deal with the record company experience and what happened?**

One thing I am still bitter about is that no-one told us that we should have a manager. We were four kids dealing with a huge international record company. We would have signed anything put before us. We didn't understand the business. We needed a manager to negotiate on our behalf, to fight our corner. He would have demanded better distribution, insisted the booking agency work harder in securing gigs. Protected us every step of the way.

As it was we simply accepted the crumbs thrown to us. So we did not get the gigs we should have had. It is incredible that we never played the Roundhouse or the UFO club. Yes we did get some good club and college gigs but never enough.

But having said that, we enjoyed the recording side of our career more than the endless hours trundling up and down England's fledgling motorway system to play to drunk students or a bunch of rockers in the back room of a pub.

Our home was the vast Fontana/Philips number one recording studio at Stanhope Place just by Marble Arch. I have so many fond memories of all-night sessions in that studio, crafting our songs, singing our harmonies as a group together at the microphone. The darkened studio, the twinkling lights in the control room, Dick's enthusiasm as the tracks took shape, the loud playback that literally took your breath away.

And of course, we were very fortunate that in spite of the fact that we had had no chart success, Dick insisted that the company invest in more studio time to record a second album, *Faintly Blowing*. Someone did tell us that Dick had told them that he was convinced he had "the new Beatles." Very flattering, but sadly his dream failed to materialize.

**How did you move from music to visual artwork?**
If I had not been involved in music I would have loved to paint or be involved in design of some kind. My brother is a wonderful artist and never stops painting.

My interest is in photography and design. I can't paint. When I am at home and not involved in musical activities my passion is photography. You can see my work at 500px.com under the name Link Bekka.

**How do you find working between the mediums of music and visual composition? Is it the same or do you need to be more open to collaboration with people, say, in music rather than painting?**

I love collaborating with other musicians! I have released three album with the amazingly talented Damien Youth. He and I became musical brothers with the very first songs we wrote together. It was weird how we were so in tune with each other's understanding of where we wanted to go in our collaboration. Our concept album, *Nevergreen*, can be ordered from chelsearecords.co.uk and *Tattoo* can be ordered from rocketgirl. co.uk and our band album, *The Morning Set*, can be ordered from gragroup.com/daltrey.html

And just out this very week is my album written and recorded with a great new-psyche band called The Asteroid #4. Order it on Amazon.

But I also enjoy the solitary experience of taking photographs which I can then develop digitally. The process can take many hours of work. But I do like the peace and quiet of working alone. I also very much enjoy designing the artwork for my albums all of which can be ordered from chelsearecords.co.uk.

**It's been said Kaleidoscope and Fairfield Parlour are definitive favorites of lost sounds of the '60s. Yet people keep returning to these lost sounds like you working with Joel Gion from BJM recently and other musicians seeking you out. How do you define how your sound was first received, then it fell into a deep slumber for a while, and how it has regained relevance and inspired modern musicians today?**

I have no idea how this new appreciation of our work has emerged, how time has proven to be our friend. But I am humbled by the attention of new generations of musicians who tell me they find so much of interest in our work.

When originally released this music slipped under the radar through poor distribution. We were simply unlucky to have signed to a lousy record company and not had someone to guide us through the dark alleys of the corporate world of music, where executives were only interested in profit, having no appreciation of the music and very little respect for their artists.

But I'm not going to whine on about that. Look, I'm just happy that after an incredible half-century we are remembered at all! The fact that people still come up to me at gigs, as they did last night at the Austin Psych Fest pre-party, and tell me how much they love these old songs is reward enough for all that heartache of so long ago.

**You've collaborated with The Asteroid #4 recently, it's been said you have meticulously high standards—how did you find working with this band and fusing with their musical vision?**
We connected immediately. They punted the tracks across the ether in mp3 form. I then spent some time getting to know the music before working out a melody line and lyrics. I then recorded a scratch vocal and buzzed it back across the ocean. When I was playing in California in late 2011 we cut the lead vocals at Rob Campenella's L.A. studio.

I am immensely pleased with the resulting album, *The Journey*. The band is so good and the guys themselves are great characters and simply nice people. We have been meeting up briefly during my stops on this current tour. We are all excited about the album and hope it will reach a wide audience.

**What future projects are in the works for you, events, musical collaborations and possible exhibitions?**
Damien and I are working on a fourth album which I am very excited about. Ryan of Asteroid #4 did say last night that it would be good to work with the band on a second album. Wow! That would be good.

After this tour I will need a rest. Although mentally I am still a twenty-five year old when I look in the mirror, I realize I am not! I have enjoyed playing live again with my great band of crazy American musicians, but I ain't getting any younger. I have so much I still want to do but the sand is slipping away. Over the last couple of years l have been writing about my old band and currently have six books available to purchase online at blurb.com.

I am now working on a seventh, which will chronicle the writing and recording process for *The Journey*. I keep busy! I stay happy. I am content.

*Published: The Wild Magazine, May 2013*

# Saul Williams

## Saul Williams Talks Martyr Loser King, Hackers and Drones

Saul Williams is a veteran poet, actor, musician and writer who has been infiltrating international artistic communities for nearly 20 years. The multitalented artist starred in the award-winning indie film *Slam* in 1998, performed in the Broadway hip-hop musical *Holler If You Hear Me*, and has released six books and seven albums throughout the span of his career. Still, Williams continues to embark on an exploration to create new experiential art projects.

His latest endeavor, a graphic novel and album entitled *Martyr Loser King*, is an exploration of Williams' fascination with hacker culture, art, technology, feminism and finding new ways to connect with the world's evolving youth culture. We caught up with Williams ahead of his April 25 performance at Slim's to talk about his new work, drones, why hacking is not voyeurism, and several books he's been reading to find inspiration for his new project.

\* \* \*

**Your new graphic novel and album, *Martyr Loser King*, is a concept you have been talking about since 2013. When was the actual moment the concept became realized in your imagination?**

The moment the idea clicked for me was after I read this graphic novel named *Habibi* by Craig Thompson. At the time the story of a hacker was kind of floating in my mind but I was uncertain as to how I wanted to tell it. The graphic novel opened me up to how I would tell the story using that format, and it informed me on how I would make the music. I started writing the words and the music for it as a graphic novel, as opposed to a book of poetry. The breakthrough for the music came from living in Paris and being exposed to a lot of different kinds of music and a lot of different people. I traveled to Africa while I was based in Paris because it was way more accessible. I was encountering a lot of kids and cell phones were everywhere. IPhones were everywhere. Technology was everything. Africa as a continent has the highest number of people connected to the internet because of its size. It is also the only continent where the majority of people are under 25. I realized, "Ok, this is who I have to talk to."

**What's your interpretation of a hacker?**

I think of disruption. It's the modern way of disrupting the norm. A hack is something that makes life easier. It is a shortcut. I hack by writing poetry. I'm coding the decoding in poetry. I'm finding new codes and shorter ways to output ideas quicker through poetry—hacking ideas, hacking frames of thought and references. I've been doing that for years. It doesn't only belong to what we relate it to in terms of computers.

I was reading a book *Testo Junkie* by Beatriz Preciado and she considers herself a "gender hacker." It's about a woman who injects herself with testosterone every day to feel the effects. There are all these ways of unwiring, rewiring, dewiring systems of thought and systems of being.

**Do you look at hacking as voyeurism or an act of war?**

Are those my only two options? [laughs]

**Yes, for this question.**

In my sense of it, hacking is not voyeurism—for example, a life hack can be as simple as finding a simpler way to tie your shoes. In terms of an act of war, I see hacking as a means of stopping or pausing acts of war. When I look at someone like Edward Snowden—better yet let's look at Aaron Swartz—that doesn't fit into voyeurism or an act of war. Downloading those books free from MIT and being given 13 felonies by the US government when he should be on the cover of *New York Times* as the future of America as one of its most promising pupils. Instead he committed suicide at the age of 26.

The act of war is set against the hacker because they're trying to set the standard, and they don't want us to go against it.

**Maybe war was a bit of a dramatic word. What about it being used with a level of malice, like when Ben Affleck's emails were leaked, asking that he not have the news shared publicly that his ancestors owned slaves?**

Well, there are white-hat hackers, grey-hat hackers and black-hat hackers. There are hackers that do good, there are some that set themselves up just to say, "Hey, there are loopholes in the system that need to be fixed." There are hackers that set themselves up to be of aid to power structures. It's not always malicious, but it's not always benevolent.

**When you want to communicate and create a project exploring information or a topic you are interested in, do you research heavily or do you tap into an intrinsic stream of consciousness to express your ideas?**

I research and then stream. For example, I was just reading this wonderful book called *The Theory of the Drone*. It is a philosophical piece on the usage of drones. What does it mean for an act of war to not involve physical combat? What does it mean for someone to receive a medal of honor when now the form of combat is actually non-combative? They're sitting in a room hitting buttons like a video game and there is no real courage involved. What does that mean in terms of transparency and surveillance? There was enough material recorded in 2009 that it would take 24 years to view it all.

**In relation to the usage of drones to replace physical combat, and the new influx of feminine independence and fourth-wave, post-modern feminism: Do you think the usage of drones could be a way for the American patriarch to implement self-preservation of men's bodies?**

I think that men in particular are privileged on this planet. The thing about privilege is that it creates a sort of comfort where you don't really question the norm or fight against it if you don't have to. There is a sense of obliviousness or a faux obliviousness that exists. I don't think that men are particularly thinking in the ways you are expressing, although some are paid to do so, but I do think that men have a structural form of existence embedded in them that makes them want to maintain the status quo and maintain power over women in society. I think many men are heavily invested in that, whether they realize it or not.

**You're going to be performing at Slim's in San Francisco on April 25. Since we've just talked a lot about technology and cultural issues that are affecting the world and nation, will you have a message to address the local issues of displacement and the imbalance of wealth, class and the arts in San Francisco?**

I'm super aware of what's going on there. My purpose for this album is to provide what every activist needs. I want to provide that creative fuel. The best I can bring to the table is what I do best. I'm here to inspire artists and people who feel compelled to resist the gridlock that these new situations are creating. The purpose of *Martyr Loser King* is to make people realize that everyone has the capacity to bring about change and that we can do it together.

*Published: SF Weekly, April 2015*

# Talib Kweli

## Race, Class, and Compassion: Talib Kweli Straddles the Worlds of Music and Activism

Talib Kweli is perhaps the most well-known yet unknown artist in hip-hop. Determined to do away with the pompousness that's often associated with his level of celebrity, Kweli nonetheless expresses empathy for some of the more visible and pretentious hip-hop artists in the game. At the same time, his own music stands on a soapbox—one that forces society to look at itself through an unfiltered black-and-white lens—as he raps about social injustices that other musicians shy away from.

Kweli is versatile: He was part of the groundbreaking hip-hop duo Black Star along with Mos Def, and continues to release albums that paint vivid pictures of the Black American experience; helped nurture the early careers of Kanye West and J. Cole; marched and protested in Ferguson; and created music for *Game of Thrones*. In conversation, Kweli uses terms like white supremacy and compassion in the same breath. His activism is in the vein of Angela Davis, his perspective similar to that of literary giant James Baldwin. In short, Kweli is a rare rapper: He stands for service and displays a surprising level of humility.

We caught up with the Brooklyn MC as he embarked on a national tour with political rapper Immortal Technique and the Brazilian-born artist NIKO IS, whose debut, Brutus, was just released by Kweli's Javotti Media. Kweli will speak on race, justice, and hip-hop at the Castro Theatre on Friday, March 20. The rappers will perform at the Fillmore on Sunday, March 22.

\* \* \*

**Tell us about NIKO IS. Why did you choose him for this tour?**
In my career, I've been blessed to run into artists who are intel-

lectual, and fantastic, often before they blow up and become big artists. It happened with Kanye, Jay Electronica, Kendrick Lamar, and J. Cole. They're all artists I made music with before the world embraced them. NIKO, to me, is not different from the people I just named. On top of that, him being from Brazil and being able to speak three different languages, I see him as a visionary and as someone I didn't want to pass up the opportunity to work with. I think a year or two from now, people are going to be talking about NIKO IS in a big way.

**You're wearing a number of hats right now: A few weeks back you were concentrating on the work you've done with regard to the uprising in Ferguson. How do you balance your music and activism?**

It's been hard to do everything I want to do, but it's been worth it. The activism is a natural progression of my music.

**You've blamed overly militarized police forces in Ferguson for "harassing and throwing [people] in jail for exercising their right to peaceful protest." You also created the Action Support Committee, which has raised more than $100,000 to help protesters. How will you disperse those funds?**

There are 13 people in the committee that are overseeing the dispersion of the funds that were raised. There are five programs on the ground that we gave a small amount of money to. We chose programs run by young activists who are not tied to a charity system. There is still a lot of money left over. We've committed ourselves to distributing all of it by fall of this year. We want to be strategic, and not just run through it all in three weeks. I also want to be clear that there have been a lot of blogs and stuff written about what we're doing with the Ferguson Defense Fund, but the only thing that is official is what the Action Support Committee actually released; the press release which is on my Tumblr page.

**There are a number of hip-hop musicians who chose not to speak up about Ferguson. What drove you to support the protesters?**

I know the mainstream media is controlled by six corporations and their job is to tell the story of the officials. I realized what the people on the street were saying was different than what I was hearing on the news. That made me want to go. I also understand that people trust me to give an honest perspective on what's going on in situations like this.

What I saw was crazy. I had cops throw me on the ground and put guns in my chest, and that's why I speak so passionately about this. I'm not a violent person. I was walking in the streets with the people and it happened to me too. It had nothing to do with me being a celebrity, but I thought it was important as an artist who has said the things I've said on my records to go to Ferguson and not just be someone who was talking about it online.

**Kanye has said that he did not speak out on the turmoil in Ferguson because his father requested that he stay out of it.**
Besides the obvious example of Kanye saying "George Bush doesn't like black people," there are other examples of him talking about class and race. He's a friend of mine. I definitely don't agree with everything he says, but I think 95 percent of what he says is incredibly accurate. There are other things he goes through that I can't relate to. I can still ride the train and walk down the street; not everyone recognizes me. I cannot imagine what he goes through and the sacrifices he has to make when it comes to what he chooses to say and what he doesn't.

**Lately, there has been a string of shootings at high-profile hip-hop shows—Chris Brown, Nicki Minaj, and T.I. shows, just in the past few months. Do you think violence at live hip-hop events is increasing?**
In my personal experience, I don't feel like there has been uptick in the amount of shootings at shows where large gatherings of disenfranchised people are at. I mean, in the jazz era, people were getting sliced up at jazz and blues shows and now it's happening in hip-hop. You have artists like Chris Brown and Nicki Minaj

who have poor, disenfranchised young people of color coming out to gather in large places. There's a lot of anger and tension at the shows and these things happen. I think these are more social things than the effect of the actual music. The music might be the product of those environments, but not the cause. Due to social media, we have increased coverage of these issues, which makes it look like the shootings are more frequent.

**What are you focusing on right now?**

Throughout my whole career, my focus has been around the prison-industrial complex and it being the most effective tool for white supremacy. I came up in the crack era of the '80s. The crack comes from this whole mandate that was developed since slavery to Jim Crow to when Nixon was in office to what changed the Democrats down South to Republicans. Law and order and the criminalization of young people of color and for-profit prisons all serve the same thing, which is maintaining white supremacy. The phrase "white supremacy" has been largely removed from context largely due to guilt, and I wish there was a more accurate term, but I think anything else at this point in history would be inaccurate. White supremacy is the father of racism and I think it's even the reason why we are having a discussion on class. That's what I find myself mostly pushing back against.

I am a human being first and to me, humanity is about compassion. The thing I see myself being most compassionate about is poor people.

*Published: SF Weekly, March 2015*

# Tech N9ne

## The Karmic Concepts of Tech N9ne

I pissed Tech N9ne off right away. I got my time zones mixed up and was in the bathroom brushing my teeth when he called. I hit him back three minutes later and he, with good reason, answered the phone with a stern "Yeah." I apologized in a terrified tone and told him I was really sorry for missing his call. He laughed and comforted me saying he'd just woken up himself.

I wanted to interview rapper Tech N9ne, whose real name is Aaron Dontez Yates, because I think he is one of the most powerful independent artists on the planet. Tech is the king of misanthropic, Midwestern hip-hop. Born and raised in Kansas City, Missouri, the MC has built a strong and passionate connection with his horde of fans since his start in the late '90s by making music that is too Black for the Juggalos, but too hick for Wu-Tang fans. He's sold more than 1.8 million records independently, and last year he broke the record for the longest tour in hip-hop history, playing 90 shows in 99 days. This spring, he's embarking on the Independent Powerhouse Tour with Brotha Lynch Hung, Krizz Kaliko, Kutt Calhoun, Rittz, and Ces Cru to promote his new album, *Something Else*, which will be released on June 25.

Despite our rocky start, I got Tech to talk about some interesting stuff. We discussed his friendship with Lil' Wayne, and he taught me some wonderful new slang like the word "fuckboy." Enjoy!

\* \* \*

**Are you a workaholic? Do you have time-management issues? Do you sleep?**
I don't sleep [laughs]. Nah, yes I do. I have to get my eight hours

in or what I do wouldn't be possible. I have to have sleep in order to move like we move—we're like the military. We do shows, we put albums together, we put out samplers, we do commercials, and we do movies now—you have to get rest for that. But we still have a long way to go. There are a lot of places we haven't been.

**What made you decide to go on tour just a year after your recording-breaking, 99-show Hostile Takeover Tour?**

Every time we put out albums, we have to go on tour to support our album, and I put out albums all year long. The only reason why I didn't do another domestic tour was because I was in Europe and Canada. So I haven't stopped touring, I've just been playing shows in other countries. I have a new album coming out called *Something Else* and all the other acts on the tour have albums coming out, so we're trying to support them.

**How do you choose your artists for the tour? Do you choose artists just by the fact that they're putting out records or do you handpick them for their talent?**

I choose all of them carefully. I chose them to be elite, so when it comes to making albums, I don't have a problem with them. When it comes to touring, I don't have to baby-sit any of them.

**Your latest single featuring T-Pain is titled "B.I.T.C.H." I'm a feminist, so I don't really like that it's called that, but…**

[N9ne interrupts me, slightly agitated] It's called "Breaking In To Colored Houses." T-Pain and I have worked together, like, three times. We did a track on my last album, "All 6's and 7's," with Lil' Wayne. We also did one for his *Stoic* mixtape and now this song because that's my brother and I love what he does.

**Do you and Wayne have a lot in common? You two basically have the same job.**

Yeah, we're real dudes. Right before I called you, I was about to text him and say, "I'm glad you're OK, boy." He always texts me back, he's a real guy. That's what we have in common. We also have stress in common, and with stress comes a lot of other things. Everybody has stress. That's what we deal with as human beings. So whenever one of us is having stress, we hit each other up and go, "Are you OK? You good?"

**Do you think moguls like you, Wayne, and Birdman are a bit more down-to-Earth and have more camaraderie between you than other label CEOs who are not also rappers and super-intimidating Black men?**

If you're real, you get real results from other real people. If you ain't no bitch, or you ain't no shyster, you'll always get respect. I get respect because I give respect. I'm not shysty, so I don't have shysty motherfuckers around me. When I meet Rick Ross, when I meet Baby, when I meet Chino from the Deftones, when I meet Corey Taylor from Slipknot, when I meet Travis Barker, when I meet Jay-Z, when I run into these people, they are respectful. And I am, too. If they sense there was a bitch in me, it probably wouldn't be that way. If people would just be themselves, they would have camaraderie with other people like we do. But not everyone is built to be 100 percent man.

**So you're saying you never run into asshole business people or negative people?**

I've run into some throughout my journey, but we don't fuck with them. When people show you their colors, you stay away, and you don't go backwards. We try not to keep fuckboys around us, you know?

**I'm not sure what your religion is, but it sounds like you have a very simple karmic idea about life, friends and business.**

Totally. I was raised a Christian. My mom married a Muslim when I was 12. I ran away from home when I was 17 and I've been on the streets ever since. I didn't run away from home because I didn't have love, I ran away from home because I was confused and there's nothing wrong with being confused. When you're confused, you try to figure out what the fuck you're confused about, and knowledge comes from that.

**You have any advice for young rappers who want to succeed in the game?**

Everybody thinks they have rhythm. But that's not the case. If you're going to succeed in music, rhythm is one thing you have to have. But you know, there's technology now called Pro Tools that will make you sound like you have rhythm. Technology makes it easier for young people, nowadays. We didn't have that back in the day. But now, we see how easy it is to sound good when you don't. So I say to the young people who are trying to do music, just make sure you have those extremely beautiful pulses. When I say pulses, I mean beats. Without a pulse, there is no life. First they listen to the pulse, then they listen to what you're saying.

**That's good advice. Are you excited about the Independent Powerhouse Tour you're on right now?**

This is the best lineup we've had in a long time. I wish I could watch the whole show. These acts that we have on the label right now make me want to get dressed and get my face painted early just so I can watch the whole show. That's a big thing.

**And you're not trying to top your last history-making tour?**

I'm never going to top it. Somebody else is going to have to top it. I did my duty. I'm not doing that again [laughs].

*Published: Vice, March 2013*

# THEESatisfaction

## Hip-Hop Duo THEESatisfaction Talks Beats, Queerness and Cosmos

Stasia "Stas" Irons and singer Catherine "Cat" Harris-White make up the futuristic and Afrocentric band THEESatisfaction. The hip-hop duo are creating quite a positive stir with their new full-length album, *EarthEE*, which comes out today on Sub Pop Records. The album is dense with Stas Irons' layers of sensuous and atmospheric soundscapes warmed with Cat Harris' carefully woven blanket of jazz-influenced vocals. I talked with THEESatisfaction about their connection, their personal ideals, and their perceptions of female empowerment.

\* \* \*

**When you two performed for the first time at an open-mic night in Seattle, were you instantly aware that you two would connect and bond so strongly?**

STAS: It happened over time. Cat was a resident singer at the open mic. She knew the band who played there so every time I would go, I would see her. I wouldn't always perform when I was there because I was shy. As I kept seeing her over time I was like, "Damn, I need to talk to her."

**Were you actively searching for a singer to collaborate with or do you consider it fate?**

STAS: I would say it was fate. I never thought of myself being in an actual band. I did have visions of myself performing in stadiums, but I didn't know how I was going to get there. I was not necessarily on that path during that time. Everything lined up when Cat and I met. We both had ambitions but didn't really know how it was all going to happen.

**When you both agreed to become a musical group, what were the**

**first steps you took to compose the music and make it a reality?**
CAT: I had been singing in bands for a couple of years before I met Stas. I was a jazz vocalist singing in a bunch of jazz groups. The last group I was in before THEESatisfaction, I asked Stas to come play with us. I thought she would benefit from the experience, so I originally brought Stas in to do harmonies with me. We began to really vibe out because we liked a lot of the same music and she introduced me to a lot of music I didn't know about. I feel like I did the same for her. I really enjoyed playing with her so we played a couple of shows together without the other band. We realized we could do the music ourselves without having ten other people in the group and we also knew we could do a million different things with that freedom. Stas already had experience making beats in GarageBand, and I was already in school for music and had been involved with it all my life. We didn't have the money to go into a studio and we didn't want to pay anyone to make our beats. We wanted to be able to do everything in-house.

**How did you want to affect people with your art?**
CAT: I think we just wanted to perform together. I love to be on the stage. I always have to be on the stage and on the mic, and I'm always thinking about how I can find a way to get to the mic. I was always trying to find a way to be on stage all the time, so when Stas and I decided to do the music, I said to her, "Let's do this for real." My goal for the group was to have us perform as much as possible and have fun.

STAS: Basically, we just wanted to jam the fuck out. We wanted to sing and dance around and have fun. Also, a lot of the sounds we were making were sounds we weren't hearing. We were trying to create something that was unique and exciting. We treat it as art, but it is also about getting together, vibing out, and having a good time.

**How did you meet your friend and collaborator Ishmael Butler (of Digable Planets and Shabazz Palaces)?**

CAT: We've both been fans of Ish since the days he was in Digable Planets. I used to live in Hawaii, so my big brother would send my other brother and I music videos of current music in the '90s. I specifically remember seeing a lot of Digable Planets music videos on there. I have a really deep connection with his music and it's something I really aspire to. His music is something that really opened my mind. We ended up meeting him at a gallery at a mutual friend's event, and it was quite curious because he looked at us with a familiar eye. It was really bizarre.

STAS: Yeah, it was like two fans meeting each other. He was a fan of ours and we were big fans of his music. We knew that somehow we had to come together to see if collaborating would work, but that wasn't the first thing. We just wanted to hang out and be friends before any of the music was brought up. When we did come together in the studio, it worked out so well because a lot of people said the earlier stuff we put out reminded them of Digable. So it was really comfortable and natural for us to put music together.

**Now that you've gone from being independent to having more resources and access to production, how have things changed for you?**

CAT: Well, we still produce our own music. We don't outsource our production. Erik Blood helped us produce stuff, so we brought someone into the team, but Stas makes most of the beats and is an originator of our sound and I make beats from time to time. We haven't changed much in terms of production. A lot of [different] things you hear are just us perceiving things differently. I just wanted to make things clear because people get confused and assume, "now you have professional production and other people produce your beats."

**It's inspiring to learn that you are doing it on your own, and sets a great example for future female producers.**

CAT: Sub Pop is super awesome with letting us decide how we want our music to sound.

**How did your musical collaboration with the legendary musician, Meshell Ndegeocello, come about?**

CAT: She was sitting on a panel in Seattle and we were both out of town, but a friend of ours was there. She [Meshell Ndegeocello] was asked who was her favorite group was at the time and she said, "THEESatisfaction." Our friend tweeted us and let us know, then we went back and forth on Twitter with Meshell and exchanged information. She said, "I love you guys, maybe we should work together." And we said "Yeah!" [laughs] She's a legend and has been in this industry for quite some time. We've learned a lot from her and it's wonderful to have her on our album.

**It's understood that you two really wanted to collaborate and have fun with your music, but was there ever a time where you experienced trials and tribulations that caused you to feel like you weren't sure the music was going to work out?**

CAT: Tons! [laughs] When we started out people were weird about it. They would say, "I don't know. I don't know if I get it." There were people who were supporters, but there were definitely naysayers who said, "I don't know if that kind of hip-hop is going to make it. That's not what's popular. That's not what people want to hear." People thought the music was weird, and we've had a lot of crazy things happen over the years in regards to people and their perception of us. People have called us feminists, which is cool, but we don't cling to too many labels. We're openly queer and we like women and we want women to know that we like them. We've had our highs and lows but we don't focus on it a lot. We spent our time working and hustling to even make it this far. We took every opportunity we were given to perform at an open-mic, or went to see shows and connected with anyone we knew. I feel like Stas and I are very lucky and blessed because we were very involved in the Seattle scene within our families as we grew up. Stas had a scene and I had a scene. We were involved in different communities, so when the time came we started reaching out to folks who we knew supported us. But again, there were people saying, "Two queer hip-hop girls doing this? I don't know," or, "You guys make your own beats, maybe you should get someone else to make your beats."

**What do you think about modern feminism and do you connect with it in any way?**

CAT: My dad is a feminist. I feel like I am a strong woman so I don't really need to use the term. I want the best for women around the world. I'm not familiar with many of the feminist issues going on right now, but I know that there are a lot of strong and amazing women who are acting, making music, and leading right now. Queer and trans woman are doing amazing and groundbreaking work in the world of art. There's more of a place for women in the arts now, especially for women of color and Black women to be free and to express themselves. I guess that would feed into what modern feminism is, even with the return of Sleater-Kinney and what they're going on Sub Pop. And Broad City, everything they do on stage is so extreme and they are super open about being themselves. I think it is a new time. I don't feel like there will ever be a time where feminism won't be needed. It is a proclamation of female empowerment. I think it's a really amazing time to be a woman.

**Your music is reminiscent of Black experimental art-house music and hip-hop like Gil Scott Heron, Sun Ra, Afrikka Bumbatta, etc. Do these kinds of artists from the past influence you?**

STAS: Yeah, all day. That's the kind of music we vibe out to naturally. The fact that you picked up on that in our music is great. We listened to a lot of Sun Ra during the creation of this record along with a lot of P-Funk Parliament. We also watched the "Cosmos" series with Neil deGrasse Tyson and he talked a lot about climate change and how vast the universe is. I think that's how we wanted our album to feel. We wanted to take you away from this planet to make your realize how small, and at the same time, how big we are.

**What would you like for your fans and listeners to know about this album?**

STAS: One thing a lot of people don't know is that this album is our break-up album. We haven't broken up as THEESatisfaction, but Cat and I were a couple and now we're not. This album was therapeutic and healing. It was also very hard to put together because of the head spaces that we were in. The fact that this came together means a lot to me and I love it because of that. I know it is going to touch a lot of people in that way as well.

CAT: Yeah, it was definitely a healing process and a self-assurance project for sure. We were reflecting and looking back and it was a relaxing and rejuvenating project.

*Published: Bitch Magazine, February 2015*

# Thank Yous and Acknowledgements

**Publications:**
Aquarium Drunkard
Bitch Magazine
Broke-Ass Stuart
Colorado Springs Independent
East Bay Express
Hooded Utilitarian
MTV Iggy
New York Amsterdam News
Publik / Private
SF Bay Guardian
SF Station
SF Weekly
The Wild Magazine

**Editors:**
Justin Gage
Bill Forman
Stuart Schuffman
Sarah Mirk
Sam.Lefebvre
Noah Berlatky
Isabela Raygoza
Kristin Fayne-Mulroy
Emma Silvers
Matt Saincome
Blaine Skrainka
Wilbert Cooper
Matt Crawford

**Publicists/label management:**
Bekah Zietz
Jenna Rosen
Stephanie Weiss
Steve Kille
Stuart Flint
Tiffany Mea
Judy Miller Silverman
Stuart Flint
Anton Newcombe
Lisa Barton
Christoph
Abby Reutzel
Sub Pop Records
Xemu Records
A Recordings Ltd

**Artists:**
Alice Coltrane
Blaze Foley
Rowland S. Howard
Lydia Lunch
Spiritualized
Gary Wilson
Psychic Jiu-Jitsu
Panda Bear
Earl Sweatshirt
Shabazz Palaces
Kendrick Lamar
Pink Mountaintops
J. Mascis
Betty Carter
Angelique Kidjo
Saul Williams

Jo Mersa Marley

THEESatisfaction

Christopher Owens

Talib Kweli

Ishamel Butler

Peter Daltrey

Jason Simon

Jodie Smith

Tech N9ne

**Special Thanks:**

John T. Harvey Jr.

Chris Parsons

Jeremy Belcher

Christine Rose Infanger

Ryan McBride

Chris Phillips

Amber Davis

Kiasha Bennet

Jewel Lennon

Dan Breen

Kate Porter

Gina Denton

Breck Brunson

Celeste Obomsawin

Sonny Pearce

Nicole Vranas

Kyle DeMartini

Kevin Lehner

Contemporary culture has eliminated both the concept of the
public and the figure of the intellectual. Former public spaces –
both physical and cultural – are now either derelict or colonized
by advertising. A cretinous anti-intellectualism presides,
cheerled by expensively educated hacks in the pay of
multinational corporations who reassure their bored readers
that there is no need to rouse themselves from their interpassive
stupor. The informal censorship internalized and propagated by
the cultural workers of late capitalism generates a banal
conformity that the propaganda chiefs of Stalinism could only
ever have dreamt of imposing. Zer0 Books knows that another
kind of discourse – intellectual without being academic, popular
without being populist – is not only possible: it is already
flourishing, in the regions beyond the striplit malls of so-called
mass media and the neurotically bureaucratic halls of the
academy. Zer0 is committed to the idea of publishing as a
making public of the intellectual. It is convinced that in
the unthinking, blandly consensual culture in which we live,
critical and engaged theoretical reflection is more important
than ever before.

# ZERO BOOKS

*If this book has helped you to clarify an idea, solve a problem or extend your knowledge, you may like to read more titles from Zero Books. Recent bestsellers are:*

**Capitalist Realism** Is there no alternative?
*Mark Fisher*
An analysis of the ways in which capitalism has presented itself as the only realistic political-economic system.
**Paperback:** November 27, 2009 978-1-84694-317-1 $14.95 £7.99.
**eBook:** July 1, 2012 978-1-78099-734-6 $9.99 £6.99.

**The Wandering Who?** A study of Jewish identity politics
*Gilad Atzmon*
An explosive unique crucial book tackling the issues of Jewish Identity Politics and ideology and their global influence.
**Paperback:** September 30, 2011 978-1-84694-875-6 $14.95 £8.99.
**eBook:** September 30, 2011 978-1-84694-876-3 $9.99 £6.99.

**Clampdown** Pop-cultural wars on class and gender
*Rhian E. Jones*
Class and gender in Britpop and after, and why 'chav' is a feminist issue.
**Paperback:** March 29, 2013 978-1-78099-708-7 $14.95 £9.99.
**eBook:** March 29, 2013 978-1-78099-707-0 $7.99 £4.99.

**The Quadruple Object**
*Graham Harman*
Uses a pack of playing cards to present Harman's metaphysical system of fourfold objects, including human access, Heidegger's indirect causation, panpsychism and ontography.
**Paperback:** July 29, 2011 978-1-84694-700-1 $16.95 £9.99.

**Weird Realism** Lovecraft and Philosophy

*Graham Harman*

As Hölderlin was to Martin Heidegger and Mallarmé to Jacques Derrida, so is H.P. Lovecraft to the Speculative Realist philosophers.

**Paperback:** September 28, 2012 978-1-78099-252-5 $24.95 £14.99.

**eBook:** September 28, 2012 978-1-78099-907-4 $9.99 £6.99.

**Sweetening the Pill** or How We Got Hooked on Hormonal Birth Control

*Holly Grigg-Spall*

Is it really true? Has contraception liberated or oppressed women?

**Paperback:** September 27, 2013 978-1-78099-607-3 $22.95 £12.99.

**eBook:** September 27, 2013 978-1-78099-608-0 $9.99 £6.99.

**Why Are We The Good Guys?** Reclaiming Your Mind From The Delusions Of Propaganda

*David Cromwell*

A provocative challenge to the standard ideology that Western power is a benevolent force in the world.

**Paperback:** September 28, 2012 978-1-78099-365-2 $26.95 £15.99.

**eBook:** September 28, 2012 978-1-78099-366-9 $9.99 £6.99.

**The Truth about Art** Reclaiming quality

*Patrick Doorly*

The book traces the multiple meanings of art to their various sources, and equips the reader to choose between them.

**Paperback:** August 30, 2013 978-1-78099-841-1 $32.95 £19.99.

**Bells and Whistles** More Speculative Realism

*Graham Harman*

In this diverse collection of sixteen essays, lectures, and interviews Graham Harman lucidly explains the principles of

Speculative Realism, including his own object-oriented philosophy.
**Paperback:** November 29, 2013 978-1-78279-038-9 $26.95 £15.99.
**eBook:** November 29, 2013 978-1-78279-037-2 $9.99 £6.99.

**Towards Speculative Realism: Essays and Lectures** Essays and Lectures
*Graham Harman*
These writings chart Harman's rise from Chicago sportswriter to co founder of one of Europe's most promising philosophical movements: Speculative Realism.
**Paperback:** November 26, 2010 978-1-84694-394-2 $16.95 £9.99.
**eBook:** January 1, 1970 978-1-84694-603-5 $9.99 £6.99.

**Meat Market** Female flesh under capitalism
*Laurie Penny*
A feminist dissection of women's bodies as the fleshy fulcrum of capitalist cannibalism, whereby women are both consumers and consumed.
**Paperback:** April 29, 2011 978-1-84694-521-2 $12.95 £6.99.
**eBook:** May 21, 2012 978-1-84694-782-7 $9.99 £6.99.

**Translating Anarchy** The Anarchism of Occupy Wall Street
*Mark Bray*
An insider's account of the anarchists who ignited Occupy Wall Street.
**Paperback:** September 27, 2013 978-1-78279-126-3 $26.95 £15.99.
**eBook:** September 27, 2013 978-1-78279-125-6 $6.99 £4.99.

**One Dimensional Woman**
*Nina Power*
Exposes the dark heart of contemporary cultural life by examining pornography, consumer capitalism and the ideology of women's work.

**Paperback:** November 27, 2009 978-1-84694-241-9 $14.95 £7.99.
**ebook:** July 1, 2012 978-1-78099-737-7 $9.99 £6.99.

## Dead Man Working
*Carl Cederstrom, Peter Fleming*
An analysis of the dead man working and the way in which
capital is now colonizing life itself.
**Paperback:** May 25, 2012 978-1-78099-156-6 $14.95 £9.99.
**ebook:** June 27, 2012 978-1-78099-157-3 $9.99 £6.99.

## Unpatriotic History of the Second World War
*James Heartfield*
The Second World War was not the Good War of legend. James
Heartfield explains that both Allies and Axis powers fought for
the same goals - territory, markets and natural resources.
**Paperback:** September 28, 2012 978-1-78099-378-2 $42.95 £23.99.
**ebook:** September 28, 2012 978-1-78099-379-9 $9.99 £6.99.

*Find more titles at www.zero-books.net*